Publisher's Foreword

Dear HowExpert Reader,

HowExpert publishes quick 'how to' guides on all topics from A to Z by everyday experts.

At HowExpert, our mission is to discover, empower, and maximize everyday people's talents to ultimately make a positive impact in the world for all topics from A to Z...one everyday expert at a time!

All of our HowExpert guides are written by everyday people just like you and me, who have a passion, knowledge, and expertise for a specific topic.

We take great pride in selecting everyday experts who have a passion, real-life experience in a topic, and excellent writing skills to teach you about the topic you are also passionate about and eager to learn.

We hope you get a lot of value from our HowExpert guides, and it can make a positive impact on your life in some way. All of our readers, including you, help us continue living our mission of positively impacting the world for all spheres of influences from A to Z.

If you enjoyed one of our HowExpert guides, then please take a moment to send us your feedback from wherever you got this book.

Thank you, and we wish you all the best in all aspects of life.

Sincerely,

BJ Min
Founder & Publisher of HowExpert
HowExpert.com

PS...If you are also interested in becoming a HowExpert author, then please visit our website at HowExpert.com/writers. Thank you & again, all the best!

COPYRIGHT, LEGAL NOTICE AND DISCLAIMER:

COPYRIGHT © BY HOWEXPERT™ (OWNED BY HOT METHODS). ALL RIGHTS RESERVED WORLDWIDE. NO PART OF THIS PUBLICATION MAY BE REPRODUCED IN ANY FORM OR BY ANY MEANS, INCLUDING SCANNING, PHOTOCOPYING, OR OTHERWISE WITHOUT PRIOR WRITTEN PERMISSION OF THE COPYRIGHT HOLDER.

DISCLAIMER AND TERMS OF USE: PLEASE NOTE THAT MUCH OF THIS PUBLICATION IS BASED ON PERSONAL EXPERIENCE AND ANECDOTAL EVIDENCE. ALTHOUGH THE AUTHOR AND PUBLISHER HAVE MADE EVERY REASONABLE ATTEMPT TO ACHIEVE COMPLETE ACCURACY OF THE CONTENT IN THIS GUIDE, THEY ASSUME NO RESPONSIBILITY FOR ERRORS OR OMISSIONS. ALSO, YOU SHOULD USE THIS INFORMATION AS YOU SEE FIT, AND AT YOUR OWN RISK. YOUR PARTICULAR SITUATION MAY NOT BE EXACTLY SUITED TO THE EXAMPLES ILLUSTRATED HERE; IN FACT, IT'S LIKELY THAT THEY WON'T BE THE SAME, AND YOU SHOULD ADJUST YOUR USE OF THE INFORMATION AND RECOMMENDATIONS ACCORDINGLY.

THE AUTHOR AND PUBLISHER DO NOT WARRANT THE PERFORMANCE, EFFECTIVENESS OR APPLICABILITY OF ANY SITES LISTED OR LINKED TO IN THIS BOOK. ALL LINKS ARE FOR INFORMATION PURPOSES ONLY AND ARE NOT WARRANTED FOR CONTENT, ACCURACY OR ANY OTHER IMPLIED OR EXPLICIT PURPOSE.

ANY TRADEMARKS, SERVICE MARKS, PRODUCT NAMES OR NAMED FEATURES ARE ASSUMED TO BE THE PROPERTY OF THEIR RESPECTIVE OWNERS, AND ARE USED ONLY FOR REFERENCE. THERE IS NO IMPLIED ENDORSEMENT IF WE USE ONE OF THESE TERMS.

NO PART OF THIS BOOK MAY BE REPRODUCED, STORED IN A RETRIEVAL SYSTEM, OR TRANSMITTED BY ANY OTHER MEANS: ELECTRONIC, MECHANICAL, PHOTOCOPYING, RECORDING, OR OTHERWISE, WITHOUT THE PRIOR WRITTEN PERMISSION OF THE AUTHOR.

ANY VIOLATION BY STEALING THIS BOOK OR DOWNLOADING OR SHARING IT ILLEGALLY WILL BE PROSECUTED BY LAWYERS TO THE FULLEST EXTENT. THIS PUBLICATION IS PROTECTED UNDER THE US COPYRIGHT ACT OF 1976 AND ALL OTHER APPLICABLE INTERNATIONAL, FEDERAL, STATE AND LOCAL LAWS AND ALL RIGHTS ARE RESERVED, INCLUDING RESALE RIGHTS: YOU ARE NOT ALLOWED TO GIVE OR SELL THIS GUIDE TO ANYONE ELSE.

THIS PUBLICATION IS DESIGNED TO PROVIDE ACCURATE AND AUTHORITATIVE INFORMATION WITH REGARD TO THE SUBJECT MATTER COVERED. IT IS SOLD WITH THE UNDERSTANDING THAT THE AUTHORS AND PUBLISHERS ARE NOT ENGAGED IN RENDERING LEGAL, FINANCIAL, OR OTHER PROFESSIONAL ADVICE. LAWS AND PRACTICES OFTEN VARY FROM STATE TO STATE AND IF LEGAL OR OTHER EXPERT ASSISTANCE IS REQUIRED, THE SERVICES OF A PROFESSIONAL SHOULD BE SOUGHT. THE AUTHORS AND PUBLISHER SPECIFICALLY DISCLAIM ANY LIABILITY THAT IS INCURRED FROM THE USE OR APPLICATION OF THE CONTENTS OF THIS BOOK.

COPYRIGHT BY HOWEXPERT™ (OWNED BY HOT METHODS)
ALL RIGHTS RESERVED WORLDWIDE.

HowExpert Guide to Playing Guitar

101+ Tips to Choosing, Maintaining, and Learning How to Play the Guitar for Beginners

HowExpert with Norm Fernandez

Copyright HowExpert™
www.HowExpert.com

For more tips related to this topic, visit HowExpert.com/guitar

Recommended Resources

- HowExpert.com – Quick 'How To' Guides on All Topics from A to Z by Everyday Experts.
- HowExpert.com/free – Free HowExpert Email Newsletter.
- HowExpert.com/books – HowExpert Books
- HowExpert.com/courses – HowExpert Courses
- HowExpert.com/clothing – HowExpert Clothing
- HowExpert.com/membership – HowExpert Membership Site
- HowExpert.com/affiliates – HowExpert Affiliate Program
- HowExpert.com/jobs – HowExpert Jobs
- HowExpert.com/writers – Write About Your #1 Passion/Knowledge/Expertise & Become a HowExpert Author.
- HowExpert.com/resources – Additional HowExpert Recommended Resources
- YouTube.com/HowExpert – Subscribe to HowExpert YouTube.
- Instagram.com/HowExpert – Follow HowExpert on Instagram.
- Facebook.com/HowExpert – Follow HowExpert on Facebook.
- TikTok.com/@HowExpert – Follow HowExpert on TikTok.

Table of Contents

Recommended Resources 2
Publisher's Foreword 3
Chapter 1: What is a Guitar? 8
   Acoustic Guitars 11
   Electric Guitars 13
   Summary 16
Chapter 2: Guitar Anatomy 17
   i. Head 18
      Tuning Machines 18
      Nut 19
   ii. Neck 20
   iii. Body 22
      Acoustic Guitar Body 23
      Electric Guitar Body 25
   Summary 29
Chapter 3: Choosing Your Guitar 30
   Acoustic Guitar 31
   Electric Guitar 33
   Summary 36
Chapter 4: Caring for Your Guitar 38
   Proper Guitar Storage 39
   Tuning Your Guitar 42
   Cleaning Your Guitar 45
   Restringing Your Guitar 46
   When to See a Professional 53
   Summary 54
Chapter 5: Holding Your Guitar 55
   Sitting With Your Acoustic Guitar 56
   Sitting With Your Electric Guitar 57
   Standing With Your Acoustic Guitar 60
   Standing With Your Electric Guitar 62
   Strumming Hand 64
   Fretting Hand 68
   Summary 71

Chapter 6: Basic Chords 72
- Chord Charts 73
- G Chord 74
- E Chord 76
- D Chord 78
- C Chord 79
- A Chord 81
- Major vs. Minor 82
- Am Chord 83
- Em Chord 84
- Dm Chord 85
- Chord Progressions 87
- Add Some Rhythm 90
- This is Not the End 91
- Summary 91

Chapter 7: Scales 93
- One Note at a Time 94
- C Major Scale (open) 96
- A Minor Pentatonic 100
- A Major Pentatonic 102
- C Major Diatonic 103
- Using Scales 105
- A Few More Techniques and Tricks 108
  - Slides 108
  - Bending and Vibrato 108
  - Hammer-Ons 109
  - Pull-Offs 111
  - Picking Techniques 112
- Summary 113

Chapter 8: Power Chords 114
- Power Chords Down the Neck 118
- Palm Muting 122
- Power Chord Progressions and Patterns 124
  - The "L" Progression 125
  - The Extended "L" Progression 126
  - The "X" Progression 127

  The "I" Progression 129
  Summary *130*
Chapter 9: Reading Guitar Tab... 132
  Summary *143*
Chapter 10: Now What? 144
Epilogue.. 156
About the Expert 160
Recommended Resources 161

Chapter 1: What is a Guitar?

I'll never forget what my mom said when I told her I wanted to play guitar. I was 15 years old. She said, "Absolutely not. You'll just give it up like you did the trumpet." Looking back on it now, I understand her hesitation. She was right. I played trumpet in the 5th-grade band, hated it, and quit about three months after I had started.

So, I did what any 15-year-old would do when mom said, "No." I went to my grandparents. My grandfather took me to a local guitar shop. He didn't know what to get me, and I certainly didn't have any clue.

Luckily, the owner of the shop knew exactly what I needed. He was an older gentleman who looked like a hippy Santa Claus. He was just as jolly, too. The shop was a tiny building, but it was bursting at the seams with guitars of every size, shape, and configuration.

The guitar shop owner handed me a big, dark brown acoustic guitar. "Sit down and hold this," he told me. It was a little awkward, but it somehow fit perfectly on my lap, resting just under my arm. I must have been grinning ear-to-ear because my grandfather said, "We'll take it."

I brought the guitar home; I was over-the-moon excited. My mother was not thrilled. She figured I'd play that guitar for a few weeks, and then it would sit in a corner and collect dust. But I was ready to prove her wrong. I was going to stick with this. Something inside me knew it.

I locked myself in my room after school every day for hours. I played and played and played.

It's been 18 years. To this day, my mom loves to come to my shows and watch me play.

It might seem like a silly question, but it is important to understand what a guitar is, where it came from, and how guitars continue to grow and evolve as instruments. Knowing all of this will help you appreciate the guitar, both as a way to create art and as a piece of art itself.

Tip 1: *A guitar is classified as a chordophone, a stringed instrument that produces sound from strings that are fixed between two points.*

A player plucks or strums the strings with one hand and presses the strings down with the fingers of the other hand. The shortening or lengthening of the strings changes the vibrational frequency creating musical notes. Other chordophone instruments include the bass guitar, banjo, mandolin, and ukulele. Many of the skills you'll learn in this book can be transferred to these other instruments! You'll learn more about that in Chapter 10, "Now What?"

Tip 2: *The roots of where the guitar came from can be traced to over 3,000 years ago!*

Ancient stone carvings in Southern Mesopotamia, now modern-day Iraq, show a stringed instrument whose shape very closely resembles that of an acoustic guitar. Other depictions of early guitar-like instruments come from the Middle Ages, in 12th century Europe and beyond. The word *guitar* has origins in many European languages, including the French *guitare*, the German *gitarre*, and the Spanish *guitarra*. In fact, Spain is where the standard idea of a guitar comes from, specifically the acoustic guitar.

Tip 3: Around the late 1800s, Spanish guitar builders (also called luthiers) figured out the proper proportions of the guitar.

These luthiers changed the size of the body and developed a pattern of wood reinforcements for the insides of the body. These reinforcements greatly improved the durability and sustainability of the guitar under the tension of the strings. These bracings in the top and back of the guitar revolutionized the instrument. It improved how the guitar sounded, the instrument's tone, projection, and volume. The guitars of this era are essentially identical to the instruments produced today.

Classical guitars sometimes referred to as Spanish guitars, use nylon strings instead of steel or nickel strings. The nylon strings are easier on the fretting hand fingers but require much more finesse with the strumming hand. Chapter 4, "Holding the Guitar," will explain more about the fretting and strumming hands.

Tip 4: Standard guitars have six strings and are either acoustic, meaning the sound projects naturally from the instrument itself, or electric, which uses electromagnetic pickups to amplify the sound to an amplifier or speaker.

There are, however, many different styles and variations between acoustic and electric guitars. The subcategories of acoustic and electric guitars depend on the construction of the guitar, the way they are played, and the type of music they are mostly used for.

Acoustic Guitars

Dreadnought style steel-string flattop acoustic guitar

Tip 5: *The most common subcategory of acoustic guitars is the steel-stringed flattop.*

You'll find steel-stringed flattop acoustic guitars hanging in almost any guitar shop. However, there are many different sizes and shapes of flattop acoustic guitars. For example, there are smaller parlor guitars and larger jumbo guitars. The size of the body will dictate the resonance and how the guitar sounds. The most common acoustic guitar body style is the dreadnought style.

Tip 6: Don't be afraid to ask the employees of your local guitar shop to try different acoustic guitars to see which one fits you best.

How a guitar sounds to you is important, but how it feels is more important. If a dreadnought-style guitar is too big for you, opt for a small orchestra or grand auditorium style.

As mentioned previously, another subcategory of the acoustic guitar is the classical or Spanish guitar. These guitars are strung with nylon strings to produce a "warmer" sound and are usually played with a technique called *fingerstyle*. As the name suggests, the strings are plucked with the fingers instead of strumming with a pick.

Fingerstyle is certainly more of an advanced technique, but that doesn't necessarily mean classical guitars can't be played with a pick. It just requires a different approach with the way you "attack" the strings.

Tip 7: In between steel-stringed flattop guitars and nylon-string classical guitars, there is a subcategory of hybrid or crossover guitars.

These guitars have both steel and nylon strings. In general, these acoustic guitars can be more accessible to beginners or guitarists more comfortable with acoustic steel string or electric guitars rather than straightforward nylon-string guitars.

Archtop guitars are another subcategory of acoustic guitar, but they are specifically for jazz or fingerstyle blues players. Archtop guitars are similar in build and look to hollowbody electric guitars but without the electronics of an electric guitar.

Electric Guitars

Electric guitar

Electric guitars have become synonymous with rock and roll, fame and fortune, talent and skill. But they certainly didn't start that way. The need for electric guitars arose as orchestras grew in size throughout the big band era. In fact, some of the first electric guitars were just archtop jazz guitars with pickups attached to them. The first patented electric guitar was designed in 1931 and sold commercially in 1932.

Electric guitars then worked pretty much the same as electric guitars do now. An electromagnetic transducer made of magnets wrapped in copper wire picks up (see where the name comes from?) the vibration of the guitar strings. The moving guitar string moves the magnetic field from the magnet and creates a current in the copper wire. That current travels through a cable plugged into the guitar and into an amplifier or other recording equipment. There are a near-infinite number of configurations, shapes, and sizes of electric guitars. But all of them generally work with these same basic principles.

Tip 8: Remember, the most important thing is how an electric guitar feels to you. Don't think that because you want to play a certain kind of music, you have to play a certain kind of guitar.

Variations on the electric guitar include solid body, chambered body, semi-acoustic or semi-hollow, full hollow body, and electric acoustic. Each can have different construction methods, bridge and tailpieces, pickup configurations, neck styles, and much more. One thing is for certain: the right guitar for you is definitely out there!

It may seem overwhelming or unnecessary for this many options when it comes to electric guitars. But think of it like different car models. Every design choice on a car has an impact on the way it feels, drives, and performs. Electric guitar models are very similar. Different woods can change the sound or tone. Pickups can be over- or under-wound to increase or decrease output, respectively. The shape of the neck will fit better in some hands over others. The endless possibilities should be exciting!

Tip 9: Remember these names: Leo Fender and Les Paul. They are the two biggest names in modern electric guitar manufacturing.

Though they didn't necessarily invent the first mass-produced electric guitars, their competing designs shaped the modern guitar industry as it exists today. The designs that those two gentlemen invented in the early 1950s still persist to this day. In fact, they are among the top-selling and most imitated guitar styles ever. So when you think of an electric guitar, the chances are that the image that pops into your mind is a guitar that either Mr. Fender or Mr. Paul designed.

After the innovations of the early 1950s, the electric guitar exploded in popularity. Compounded with the rise in guitar-driven music in popular culture, more and more companies began creating their own styles of electric guitars for the masses. Each company brought a unique vision and style for its brand.

Tip 10: *Along your guitar journey, you may find that one particular brand or guitar style inspires you.*

Follow that spark. Seek out guitarists that play guitars similar to ones you like. Research guitar brands and the artists that play those brands. You might discover something new you wouldn't have found otherwise. Always keep an open mind. Never limit yourself to one style or brand of guitar.

The evolution of the guitar continues to this day. For example, 7- or 8-string model guitars provide a wider range of frequencies to play. Compound radius necks combine different measurements along the length of the neck to make playing more comfortable. Active pickups are battery-powered and use electronic circuitry to boost the pickup's signal. Guitar pedals can be added along the signal chain to add special effects, like distortion, echo, or the infamous wah-wah.

Of course, this all goes without mentioning the evolution of the guitar amplifier. Just know that they've come a long way, and we'll help you figure out the right amplifier to get for your first electric guitar in Chapter 3, "Choosing Your Guitar."

Tip 11: *Your perfect guitar and guitar sound are out there.*

Hopefully, all of this should help you understand that the possibilities are truly limitless. It's quite literally taken thousands of years to get to this golden era of guitar technology. There is no better time to be a beginner guitarist.

Part of the fun of playing guitar is trying new things and discovering what works or what doesn't. Explore! Discover! And let's get playing!

Summary

- The earliest depictions of guitar-like instruments date back to over 3,000 years ago.
- Around the late 1850s in Spain, the standard idea of a guitar solidified.
- Acoustic guitars evolved into electric guitars around the 1930s because acoustic guitars weren't loud enough to be heard in a big band setting.
- In the 1950s, Leo Fender and Les Paul popularized the modern, mass-produced electric guitar that we know today.
- Guitar companies continue to innovate and develop the guitar to this day.
- The perfect guitar is out there for you!

Chapter 2: Guitar Anatomy

After a few months of non-stop playing with my first acoustic guitar, I had proven to my parents that I had the discipline to keep playing guitar. So I asked if I could get an electric guitar for Christmas. So that year, on Christmas morning, I unwrapped one of my presents to discover an electric guitar starter kit.

I'm pretty sure my parents bought it off QVC or some other TV shopping network. It wasn't the best guitar. The wood was of poor quality and lightweight. It wasn't properly set up, so the strings were way too high off the fretboard. The tremolo system never kept the guitar in tune.

The practice amp that came with it was the worst part. It was the size of a shoebox with a tiny speaker. Most cell phones nowadays sound way better than that practice amp did.

None of that mattered to me. I was the happiest kid on Earth. I plugged in, cranked it up, and played even harder. I felt like a real rockstar. But I still had a long way to go before I would actually be one.

All guitars, acoustic and electric, have three main parts: the headstock (or head), the neck, and the body. Each of these main parts has its own components that perform specific functions for the guitar.

i. Head

Tip 12: The guitar's headstock can be considered the "top" portion of the guitar. There are two main components of the headstock: the tuning machines and the nut.

Left: acoustic guitar headstock. Right: electric guitar headstock.

Tuning Machines

The tuning machines are where one end of the strings are attached. Tuning machines can come in several different types. Classic (or standard), vintage, or locking tuners are the most common. Classic and vintage tuners require the string to be wound several times around. Locking tuners have a peg or post inside that holds the string in place.

Tuning machines have tuning keys that allow you to tune the guitar. Turning them one way will tighten the strings, making the pitch higher. Turning them the other way will lower the pitch by loosening the strings.

Tip 13: Guitar tuners aren't always "righty tighty, lefty loosey." Usually, you'll turn the tuning key away from the body of the guitar to tighten the string. But, conversely, turning the key towards the body will loosen it.

Tuning machines can be arranged differently, depending on the shape of the headstock. There are six-in-line, where all six tuners are on one side of the headstock (see acoustic guitar headstock, and there are 3-and-3, with three tuners on one side and three on the other. Some guitars have 4-and-2, but these are much rarer.

Tip 14: Guitar strings are numbered one through six.

The bottom and thickest string is the sixth string. The top and thinnest string is the first string. It is crucial that you memorize this. Through all lessons going forward, the strings will be referenced by their assigned number. Guitarists will often use string numbers when talking about strings, as well.

<u>Nut</u>

The nut is right above the fretboard at the bottom of the headstock. This is where the strings sit at the base of the head. Guitar nuts can be made of several different kinds of material, including plastic, synthetic or actual bone, graphite, or ebony. Different materials allow the strings to vibrate differently, affecting the resonance and tone of the guitar.

Another important factor of the nut is how well the strings glide over it during tuning. A nut that isn't properly lubricated or one that has defects in the slots might cause the string to catch or "pop" while tuning the guitar.

Tip 15: Do NOT attempt to file the slots or adjust your guitar's nut without proper guidance. Incorrectly doing so can affect the height of the strings and make your guitar unplayable.

Before we move on, here's a fun fact about guitar headstocks. Guitar companies have trademarked shapes for their guitar heads. If you learn which shapes go to which guitar manufacturers, you'll be able to spot who made that guitar almost immediately!

ii. Neck

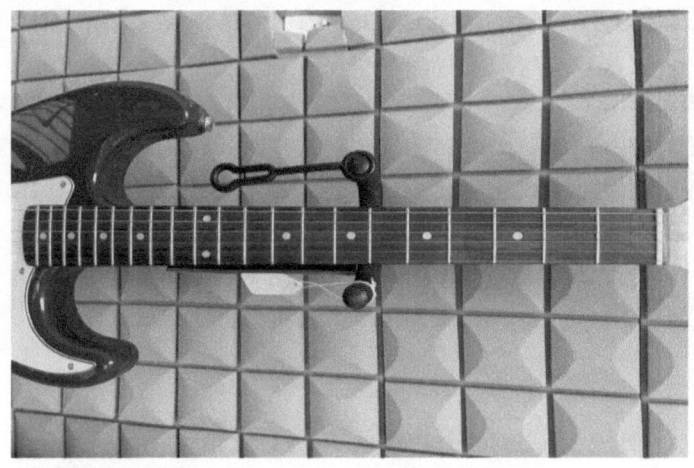

Electric guitar neck

Tip 16: The neck of the guitar is the long, slender part where the fingers of the fretting hand hold down the strings to play notes.

The wood of the neck can be made of different kinds of wood and have different finishes. The kind of wood and the kind of finish will affect how the guitar feels in the fretting hand. For example, a gloss finish may make the palm of the fretting hand "stick" better when that hand is dry. A satin finish can be more of a smooth, powdered feel. A natural finish is just sanded down bare wood.

Tip 17: Different guitars have different shaped necks. Finding the right shaped neck for you is crucial.

Some guitars have a "C" shaped neck. If you were to cut the neck parallel to the nut and look at the profile, it would be more rounded and look like a half-circle or the letter "C." Other guitars can have a "D" shaped neck. This neck shape has a flatter bottom and can be a bit wider. A "C" shaped neck is more fitting for guitarists with longer fingers. A "D" shaped neck might fit smaller hands better. But no one shape fits all. The only way to know which shape works best for you is to try them out.

The fretboard is on the front of the neck, which is separated by thin metal strips called *frets*. The term *frets* will also refer to the spaces in between two frets. So, for example, the space between the nut and the first fret is referred to as the first fret. The next space, in between the first and second, is the second fret, and so on.

Tip 18: Learn the fret markers on your guitar.

Commonly there are fret markers on the fretboard and the side of the neck. Typically, these are on the 3rd, 5th, 7th, and 12th frets. These markers will help you quickly identify frets on the neck while playing. Once you learn the fret markers, you'll know what notes you're playing at just a glance!

The fretboard itself can be made of many different materials. The most common materials are maple and rosewood. Maple fretboards are lighter in color, while rosewood fretboards are made from a darker wood. There are many other materials that fretboards can be made of, including ebony, pau ferro, laurel, and synthetic woods.

Tip 19: Just like so many other things when it comes to guitar, choosing the right fretboard wood is up to you. Start with whatever looks, sounds, and feels right. After a while, you'll be able to really appreciate the differences in these fretboards.

The differences between fretboard woods come down to two things: playability and tone. Darker woods, like ebony or rosewood, can have a tactile or rough feel to them. While that may sound like a bad thing, it can be a benefit to get a good feel of the notes while you play them. Darker woods will also have a rich, warm tone.

Lighter woods, like maple, sound crisp and bright. You might see many jazz and blues players with lighter wood on their fretboards so their guitars can "punch" through. While playing, lighter wood fretboards can feel hard and slick, even though darker woods are just as dense.

Tip 20: The actual metal portion of the frets can also come in different sizes.

You may see fret sizes listed as small, regular, medium, large, or jumbo. The sizes refer to the width and height of the metal frets, not the spaces in between the frets. For beginners, small or medium frets are the best to start with. They require less finger pressure on the string to play the note properly.

iii. Body

Up to this point, the terminology, functions, and general design between acoustic and electric guitars are about the same between headstocks and necks. However, since acoustic and electric guitars project their sounds differently, there are many differences between an acoustic guitar's body and an electric's. So we'll start with the body of an acoustic guitar first.

Acoustic Guitar Body

Acoustic guitar body

The first thing to note about acoustic guitar bodies is that they are usually much larger and thicker than electric guitars. This is because acoustic guitars need the resonance of a larger body to allow the sound to bounce around inside and then project outwards. Acoustic guitars can be made of different kinds of wood, most frequently spruce or cedar.

Soundhole

As the name suggests, this is the hole near the center of the acoustic guitar body where the sound projects out. The strings pass over this hole and vibrate when strummed or plucked. That vibration goes in the soundhole, resonates inside the body of the guitar, and then is projected out of the soundhole. Avoid blocking or plugging up the soundhole.

Tip 21: *If you play with a pick, you will at some point drop your pick in the soundhole.*

When that happens, turn your guitar with the soundhole facing down. Hold the guitar over your head and look up. Shake the guitar around and listen for the pick. Carefully shake the guitar around and try to move the pick to the soundhole. If you can get the pick to fall out of the soundhole, great! You may also have to carefully pull the pick out with your fingers. It's a hassle all guitarists are familiar with!

Bridge

The bridge is the opposite anchor point (the other being the tuning machines) where the strings start. An acoustic guitar bridge is made of the tailpiece, pins, and saddle.

Tip 22: *Acoustic guitar bridges use plastic or wooden pins to hold the strings in place.*

Do NOT attempt to pull or adjust those pins while the strings are under tension. Depending on the gauge or thickness of the strings, the bridge can hold up to 200 pounds of tension. If you were to suddenly release that tension by pulling the pins, you could damage the guitar or injure yourself. We'll get into how to change your guitar strings safely in Chapter 4, "Setting Up and Caring for Your Guitar."

The tailpiece can be made of different types of wood. Similar to the body or neck, the wood can have some influence on the tonality of the guitar. However, the tailpiece wood is generally an aesthetic choice.

The saddle is similar to the nut at the base of the neck and can be made of similar materials, like bone, synthetic bone, or plastic. Most saddles are usually set in a routed slot in the guitar's bridge. This makes it easier to take out and adjust.

Tip 23: Adjusting an acoustic guitar saddle should be done by your local guitar shop.

The saddle can be filed down and shaped to adjust how the strings sit. Taking too much material from the saddle can cause the strings to sit too low. If the strings sit too low, the guitar becomes unplayable. If the strings sit too high, it may be more difficult to press down on the strings. At that point, you may want to take your guitar in to have the saddle adjusted.

Electric Guitar Body

Two of the most popular electric guitar body shapes.

Electric guitars come in many different sizes and shapes. In general, the parts remain the same: pickups, pickup controls, bridge, and output jack.

Pickups

Tip 24: *Guitar pickups convert the vibration of the strings into electrical signals using magnets wrapped in copper wire.*

It might seem like magic, but it's really simple. The magnet creates a magnetic field that can "feel" how the strings vibrate. If you tap something metal, like a screwdriver, to the pickup, you can feel the pull of the magnet. The copper wire wrapped around it changes those vibrations into an electrical signal. That signal goes to the output jack, through an instrument cable, and into an amplifier or speaker.

Tip 25: *Many things affect how a guitar sounds, but pickups probably have the biggest impact on an electric guitar's sound.*

Pickups come in many different varieties. Single-coil pickups have a single wrapping of copper wire and generally have a brighter tone. Humbucker pickups are essentially two single-coil pickups stacked side-by-side, with the copper wires wound in opposite directions. This causes opposite polarities in the magnetic field, eliminating unnecessary noise (or bucking the hum).

Changing the pickup in your guitar is a great way to change how it sounds. Doing so requires some electrical knowledge and skill with a soldering iron. Start by playing guitars with different pickups and pickup configurations. Pay attention to how they sound clean at low volume and with high gain at high volume. Discover the differences between a "crisp, bright" pickup and one with a "warm, deep tone."

Pickups can be installed on a guitar in many different configurations, as well. For example, electric guitars can have one, two, or three pickups. The three pickup positions are bridge, mid, and neck, which describes where the pickups are placed nearest on the guitar. Some guitars have single coils in all three positions or two single coils in the neck and middle positions with a humbucker in the bridge position. Others have only two humbuckers in the neck and bridge positions.

Pickup Controls

All electric guitars have some combination of controls for the pickups. When a guitar has multiple pickups, there will be a pickup selector switch. There are 3-way switches that can select one pickup (neck, mid, and bridge) at a time. There are also 5-way switches that can run multiple pickups at once.

Tip 26: Electric guitars have volume and tone knobs to control the pickups.

The volume knob controls the output of the pickup, making it louder or quieter. Sometimes there will be multiple volume knobs that can control different pickups individually. Other times, the guitar will only have one master volume knob that controls the overall volume of all the pickups.

The tone knob will adjust the higher frequency range of the pickups. Lowering the tone knob will make the pickup sound "darker," with more mid and bottom tones. In actuality, the tone knob is a resistor to the electrical signal from the pickup. The resistance acts as a low pass filter, only allowing the lower frequency signals to pass through to the output. When the tone knob is turned up, there is little to no resistance on the pickup. As the tone knob gets turned down, you're turning down the high-end frequencies, increasing the resistance, and letting the lower frequency tones come through.

Bridge

Unlike acoustic guitars, there is a myriad of different electric guitar bridges. The function, however, is still the same. It's the opposite anchor point of the strings. On certain guitars, the strings actually pass through the body of the guitar and rest on the bridge. This is appropriately called a string-through design.

The simplest electric guitar bridge is a hardtail bridge. Just as the name implies, it's a hard and fixed point mounted to the guitar. Some hardtail bridges have two pieces (like an acoustic guitar called the saddle and tailpiece). Others have only one piece. All can be adjusted using simple tools, like a screwdriver or hex key.

The more complicated guitar bridges allow you to create vibrato by tightening or loosening the tension on the strings using what's commonly known as a "whammy bar." There are numerous styles of vibrato bridges for electric guitar. Some let you adjust the tension in only one direction, up or down; others let you go in both directions. Some utilize a locking nut system to keep the guitar in tune no matter how much you change the tension.

As with everything else involving guitar, choosing what kind of bridge you want on your guitar is up to you. For example, you might want a guitar with a locking nut vibrato system so you can do crazy "dive bomb" sounds in heavy metal guitar solos. Or you could prefer the subtler vibrato sound of a surf guitar. Figure out what kind of music you prefer and go from there.

Output Jack

Finally, on all electric guitars, there is an output jack. This is where you will plug in your ¼" guitar cable into the guitar and the other end into an amplifier. The location of the output jack will depend on the style of the guitar. The jack can be on the front or the side of the guitar. It can be flush against the body, or it can be recessed into a jack plate. Regardless, the function is always the same, and all guitars use the same ¼" cable.

Summary

- A guitar has three primary parts: the head, the neck, and the body.
- The head has two primary parts, the tuning machines (to tune the guitar) and the nut.
- The neck is where the fretboard is located and where you'll press down on the guitar strings to play notes.
- Acoustic and electric guitars have very different body styles.
- An acoustic guitar body is bigger than an electric guitar and has a sound hole to project the sound of the strings.
- An electric guitar body has pickups, electromagnetic transducers that change the vibration of the strings into electric signals.

Chapter 3: Choosing Your Guitar

I was practicing playing my electric guitar standing up in the kitchen. I had been playing and practicing for almost a year. My mother looked at me and said, "Never in a million years would I have thought you'd be a guitar player." It gave me a bit of pride to hear that, actually. I was defying parental expectations and becoming my own person, all thanks to the instrument I held in my hands.

That was when my first guitar heartbreak happened. The guitar strap I had on the guitar was cheap and flimsy. I wasn't holding the neck properly. The guitar strap slipped off, and I dropped the guitar down face first. It landed on the hard tile floor of the kitchen.

The bridge of the guitar was the first thing that hit the floor. All the tension from the strings cracked the body straight through. The guitar was ruined.

My dad and I took it to the local guitar shop. We had hoped it could be easily fixed. But, unfortunately, the guitar tech said the repair would cost more than the guitar was worth. I was devastated.

By this point, I had proven myself to my parents. They knew I was going to keep playing guitar. So, my dad offered to buy me a replacement guitar. The only catch was this would be the last one he bought for me. After that, I would have to buy my own.

It was the first time I got to choose which guitar I wanted.

Now that you've been armed with the knowledge of what a guitar is and what it's made of, the real fun can begin.

Tip 27: Choosing whether to start with an acoustic or an electric guitar is one of the most important decisions a beginner can make.

Regardless of what kind of music you want to play, you can start with either an acoustic or electric guitar. Each one has its own pros and cons. It is important to understand what those pros and cons are and how they can affect a brand-new guitarist. We'll start with the acoustic guitar's benefits and drawbacks.

Acoustic Guitar

The sound from an acoustic guitar comes naturally from the guitar itself. Because of this, you can't hide behind a cranked-up amplifier or pedal effects. Some may consider this a good thing. You really have to focus and concentrate on how you're playing when you start out in order for it to sound good. This can make you a better guitar player. On the other hand, it can also be frustrating if all you want to do is rock out when first starting.

Tip 28: Getting the right size acoustic guitar is essential.

Playing a new instrument will always feel unnatural at first. However, you should find an acoustic guitar that you can sit with comfortably. If the guitar's body is too big, you won't be able to strum properly. If it's too small, the guitar might feel like a toy instead of a proper instrument.

Recall back to Chapter 1, when we talked about different-sized acoustic guitars. The most common size is the dreadnought style, but it is by no means "one size fits all." Ask your local guitar shop to try different-sized acoustic guitars. Even if you don't know how to play a single chord, sit with the guitar on your lap and see how it feels. We'll discuss more on how to hold an acoustic guitar properly in chapter 5, "Holding the Guitar."

Tip 29: *There's no volume knob on an acoustic guitar. How hard you play is how loud you play.*

Again, there's good and bad when it comes to how loud an acoustic guitar can be. If you live in an apartment building or a house with a lot of people, it can be difficult to control how loudly you play, especially when starting out. On the flip side, learning this kind of control transfers to electric guitar, as well. You develop the skills necessary to learn dynamic strumming and picking. It's a little harder to figure those kinds of things out on an electric guitar.

Of course, all you need to start with an acoustic guitar is the guitar, a pick, and your desire to learn. It can be a little more complicated with an electric guitar. Then, you have to learn how to use your amplifier, too, the EQ settings, gain, reverb, possibly effects, etc. If you just want to pick up a guitar and start playing, an acoustic might be right for you.

Tip 30: *Acoustic guitar strings have heavier gauge strings, meaning they're thicker.*

Thicker gauge strings require more tension between the tuning machine and the bridge. This means, if you want to bend a string on a wicked guitar solo, it's much more difficult on an acoustic guitar. Thicker strings will also be more uncomfortable on the fingers of your fretting hand, at least at first. However, your hands and fingers will strengthen over time. With an acoustic guitar, your hands and fingers will become stronger than with the lighter gauge strings of an electric guitar.

In general, acoustic guitars are less expensive than electric guitars. Some beginner acoustic guitars start at around $100, but they can go up as high as $500 or $600. If you're just starting out and not sure if the guitar will be a long-term investment, you can certainly begin on a budget-priced acoustic. There is undoubtedly a difference in sound and playability within those price ranges; sometimes, you really do get what you pay for. The point is, you don't have to break the bank if you want to start playing acoustic guitar.

Electric Guitar

If your guitar heroes are more in line with bright lights, big crowds, and burning guitar solos, then you're probably going to want to start with an electric guitar. However, just like with an acoustic guitar, there are tradeoffs and benefits.

Tip 31: There are a wide variety of starter electric guitar kits to choose from.

The world of electric guitars is vast. There's nothing wrong with finding an inexpensive starter kit from a well-known guitar manufacturer when you're just starting out. These kits come with a guitar and amp and often include some accessories, like a guitar strap, cable, and picks; which starter kit you choose is entirely up to your tastes and preferences. Also, before you get too invested in your first guitar, you should bring it to your local guitar shop for a first-time setup. This will greatly improve the playability and make learning on the guitar more enjoyable.

To be sure, starter guitars may not be made of the highest-quality materials. Don't be frustrated if the guitar feels "cheap" or toy-like. Learn what you can on that instrument. Play it until you're entirely sure that you want to continue your guitar journey. Then, upgrade to a higher-quality guitar.

Tip 32: Shop around for great deals on used electric guitars.

Guitarists can sometimes be a fickle bunch. We'll purchase a piece of gear we think we want, and then once we get our hands on it, it turns out it just doesn't feel right. This means there's usually plenty of used guitars for sale.

Check online marketplaces for used guitars and guitar equipment for gear in your price range. Local guitar and pawn shops will also sometimes have used guitars on the cheap. Treasure can only be found with some digging, so do some digging to find your very own treasure!

Tip 33: Sometimes, an electric guitar is only as good as the amp it's plugged into.

One of the downsides to beginning on an electric guitar is that you must have an amp to play it through. As expensive as electric guitars can be, amplifiers can be just as, if not more, expensive. It can be just as confusing finding a good amp as finding a good guitar, which is why starter kits are often the way to go when first learning how to play.

However, don't be discouraged if your starter electric guitar amp doesn't sound as good as you'd like. Although quality has improved in recent years, to keep costs reasonable, starter guitar amps will lack the "punch" or "bite" that more expensive amps will have. Just be sure you want to play guitar for the long haul before you invest in a more expensive amplifier.

Tip 34: Electric guitar necks are typically thinner than acoustic guitars.

As you could imagine, a thinner neck makes playing an electric guitar a little easier, especially for those new guitarists with smaller hands. Also, when properly set up, the distance between the strings and the fretboard (called the "action" of the guitar) is smaller on an electric than an acoustic guitar. This means less pressure is required from the fingers of the fretting hand to play a note.

Not only are the necks thinner, but electric guitar bodies are also much slimmer than acoustic guitars. For a player who's smaller in stature, this may push them more towards an electric guitar, to begin with. Depending on the type of wood used in construction, electric guitars can also be lighter than acoustic guitars. In general, it could be said that electric guitars are more "comfortable" than acoustic guitars, especially for beginners.

Tip 35: In the acoustic versus electric debate for beginners, there really is no "wrong" answer. It ultimately comes down to two things: what you're comfortable with and what kind of music you want to play.

The skills and fundamentals of the two instruments are basically the same. In the end, the right guitar for you is going to be the one that you will stick with. If you want to start with an acoustic, then get one. If you want to start with an electric, have it. Just understand the differences and the pros and cons, as well.

Also, you won't have to stick with one over the other. Just because you start with an acoustic guitar doesn't mean you'll have to play an acoustic guitar for the rest of your life, and vice versa with an electric guitar. Play what you want to play and have fun with it!

Understand as well that the term "comfortable" is going to be a relative term. At the start, nothing will feel completely comfortable. All guitars will feel awkward and clunky. It's only through years and years of practice that you'll become "one" with the guitar.

When we talk about being comfortable, your first guitar should feel somewhat natural to you. Your fretting hand should fit nicely on the neck, with plenty of room for your fingers to move. You shouldn't have to strain or stretch with your strumming arm around an acoustic; you should have a comfortable range of motion to strum up and down. Finally, it shouldn't be so big when seated with the guitar that it takes up your whole torso.

Tip 36: Follow your inspirations and passions.

Surely, you have a preferred musical genre, or several, that you like to listen to. Perhaps you even have a specific genre or artist that inspired you to play guitar. Don't be afraid to emulate those musicians. Author Neil Gaiman once said, "Most of us only find our own voices after we've sounded like a lot of other people." Playing guitar is no different.

If you want to play like a heavy metal guitarist, maybe starting on an acoustic guitar isn't a good idea. If your passion is to be a renowned singer/songwriter, perhaps a cranked-up electric guitar won't be the best thing to get started with. Stick close to whatever speaks to your soul when you first start. Chase the spark before fanning it into a flame!

Summary

- The question is almost as old as the instrument itself: which guitar should you start with, acoustic or electric?

- Understanding the pros and cons of both kinds of guitars can help you make that decision.
- Acoustic guitars can be less expensive, and all you need is just the guitar and a pick. However, with a bigger, thicker body and heavier gauge strings, acoustic guitars can also be considered "less playable" for beginners.
- Electric guitars can be found at good deals. There are also starter packs that include the guitar and an amplifier (a must for playing electric guitar).
- Ultimately, it is entirely up to you, and there is no wrong answer. So follow your inspirations and passions, and let your musical taste be your guide.

Chapter 4: Caring for Your Guitar

I honestly don't remember when I started restringing my own guitars. I know that it took me way longer than it should have to learn how to do it on my own. I would play my guitars until the strings were almost completely rusted over, usually not bothering to get a string change until one actually broke.

In my experience, the people that own and/or operate a guitar shop are always the nicest. They're gladly willing to share their expertise. But, on the other hand, they're usually also shrewd salesmen.

This means if you're a young guitarist just starting, they'll gladly take your money to do something as simple as restringing your guitar.

I've come to find that restringing and caring for my guitars is a very therapeutic and rewarding experience. A certain Zen comes with taking care of something you genuinely enjoy and take pride in.

I pay attention to every minute detail, to the amount of grime and debris I have to clean off the fretboard, to how much tension I create on the strings, to the final polish, and to making my guitars shine.

Cleaning and restringing my guitars is now a regular routine for me before each show. An hour I set aside the day of each show to make a cup of tea, grab my gear, and enjoy the process.

Other than playing the actual show, it's usually the most enjoyable part of my day.

The guitar (both acoustic and electric) is a beautiful piece of equipment. But, in life, the things you take care of will always take care of you. So, if you're serious about playing guitar, then you should be equally as serious about taking care of your guitar.

Proper Guitar Storage

Tip 37: Always have a place to keep your guitar safe, whether that's on a stand or in a case.

All too often, guitars are just left on couches or beds. Then, someone comes along, plops down, and POP! There goes a perfectly good instrument. Treat your guitar with some respect, and have a safe place to put it.

Guitar stands are relatively inexpensive. Most work for either acoustic or electric guitars. Having your guitar on a stand in the corner of a room is an excellent place for it. If floor space is scarce (and you're allowed to put some holes in your wall), you can also opt to mount a guitar rack on your wall to hang your guitar on the wall.

Guitars mounted on the wall of a local guitar shop.

There are several different kinds of wall mounts for guitars. The simplest and most common type lets the guitar hang from the neck. They are also relatively inexpensive. Do your research and find a universal mount that works for most guitar types. Please follow the directions for whichever wall mount you choose. Nothing's worse than a guitar falling off of your wall because of a mount you didn't install properly.

Alternatively, you can keep your guitar in a case. Some guitars will come with a case when you purchase them. However, this is usually only the case with more expensive guitars. Most starter guitars will not come with a case or will only come with a gig bag.

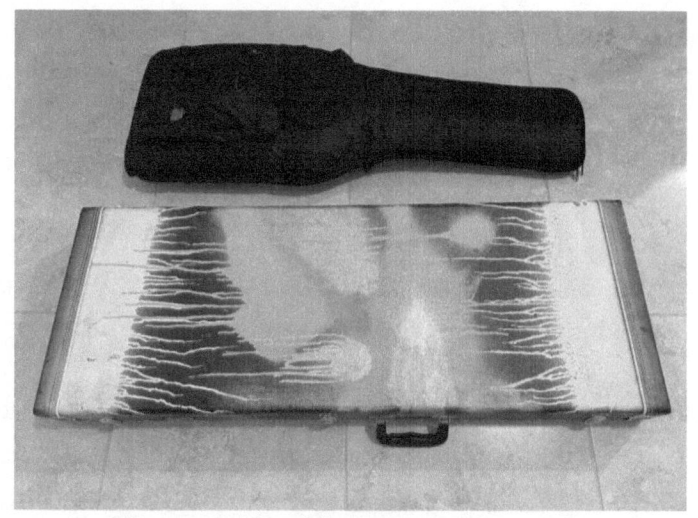

Top: Gig bag. Bottom: guitar case.

Do not mistake a gig bag for a case. A gig bag is soft and only offers protection from dirt and debris. A proper guitar case is made from pressboard or wood and is much more rigid, offering sturdier protection. A gig bag is fine for taking your guitar from place to place. But for the best protection and storage, you will want a case.

As we've already discussed, guitars come in all different shapes and sizes. So, no one guitar case fits every kind of guitar. Instead, search for your guitar body style and the case that corresponds with it. When in doubt, take your guitar to your local guitar shop and ask them what kind of case you can get.

Guitar cases are versatile for storage. Placing the guitar in the case and under your bed is a fine place. Or you can put it in a closet or storage room.

Do NOT position the case in such a way that the guitar is face down (strings on the floor) or vertically upside-down (headstock pointing down). This will ruin the guitar by placing pressure on the wrong places. Instead, the case should either have the guitar flat on its back, on its side, or with the headstock pointed upwards.

Tip 38: Guitars are made of wood and metal. Both of those materials do not do well in extreme temperatures.

Heat and humidity can cause the wood of the guitar to swell and warp, making the guitar completely unplayable. It will also rapidly deteriorate the metal portions of the guitar (strings, bridge, tuning machines, etc.). Extreme cold can also cause significant damage. The wood can shrivel and crack, completely destroying the guitar.

Do NOT leave your guitar in a car or outside for an extended period of time. Instead, the guitar should be stored indoors at room temperature (68 - 77 °F or 20 - 25 °C) with minimal humidity.

If you wind up playing your guitar outside in hot or cold weather, understand that the materials in your guitar will adjust to the temperature. Because of this, you may have to tune your guitar a few times before it stays in tune.

Tuning Your Guitar

Tip 39: Standard guitar tuning is (from lowest, thickest string to highest, thinnest string): E-A-D-G-B-E.

The easiest way to tune a guitar is to purchase a guitar tuner. Some clip on to the headstock of the guitar and "feel" the vibrations, telling you what note your guitar is playing. Others (for electric guitar and acoustic/electric guitar) allow you to plug directly into the tuner to tune your guitar. These are more accurate than the clip-on variety. They also don't pick up any interference from outside noises since the guitar is plugged directly in.

Guitar tuners. Left is a foot pedal tuner that you can plug your guitar into.

Right is a clip-on tuner that attaches to the head of your guitar.

Play the string open (without holding down any fret) and see what the tuner tells you. If a note is too low (flat), you'll need to tighten that string. SLOWLY turn the tuning key of the appropriate string to tighten it. If it goes too high (sharp), SLOWLY turn the tuning key to loosen the string. Once the tuner tells you you've hit the right note for the appropriate string, you're in tune!

You can also tune your guitar by ear. This requires some practice, and you must have your 6th string already in tune to E. You can use another instrument, like a piano or a tuning fork, or a reference note found online, to get your lowest string in tune. Play the open sixth string, listen to your reference instrument, and get the notes to sound the same. Once they sound the same, your sixth string is tuned, and you can then move on to the next.

Then, you'll play the fifth fret on the sixth string. That is an A, which is what the open fifth string should be tuned to. Play that note and the open fifth string, and tune the fifth string to match the note played on the sixth.

You repeat that process on the fifth string, playing the fifth fret on the fifth string and listening to the open fourth string, and tune the fourth string to match that note. Once the fourth string is in tune, do the same to tune the third string.

However, on the third string, you play the *fourth* fret to tune the open second string. Then, get the second string in tune, and play the fifth fret to tune the first string.

Tip 40: Depending on how old the strings are, how hard you play, or if there is a significant temperature change, you may have to tune your guitar often.

At the very least, tune your guitar each time before you start playing—no use in playing or practicing with an out-of-tune guitar. After a while, you'll be able to tell by ear if your guitar is out of tune. When in doubt, tune it up!

New strings can also take a while to stretch out and break in. Don't be frustrated if your new strings don't stay in tune. You can *gently* pull up on the strings around the twelfth fret to stretch them out. Just be careful with the thinner strings. They will break if you pull too hard.

There are several other tuning variations. Drop-D, E-Flat standard, and open G are some popular tuning variations. They are used fairly rarely and can be considered "advanced" kinds of tuning. We won't worry about that too much right now. You'll get there eventually.

Cleaning Your Guitar

Tip 41: Do NOT use regular household cleaners to clean your guitar.

Most regular household cleaners contain chemicals that can be corrosive to wood or the kinds of finish used on the guitar. Therefore, do not use glass cleaner, furniture cleaner, or all-purpose cleaner on any part of your guitar.

Various guitar cleaners

Thankfully, there are plenty of guitar-specific cleaners available for purchase. When first starting, you might want to look for guitar cleaning kits. These kits will often come with microfiber cloths and various cleaning solutions made specifically for guitar. The cleaning solutions will also be tailored for specific parts of the guitar.

Tip 42: Clean your guitar when the strings are off. This is why restringing and cleaning often go hand-in-hand.

We'll get into restringing your guitar in the next section. Also, you don't have to clean your guitar every day. Wiping it off with a clean towel after each practice or playing session is totally fine. Doing so will remove oils from your skin off of the guitar, which can often build up into dirt and grime.

Once the strings are off, take some time to clean around the fret wires. It can get pretty grimy where the fret wires meet the fretboard. Dead skin and sweat will build up in those corners. The easiest way to clean the fretwire corners is with a wooden toothpick. You can gently run a toothpick across the fret wires to scrape off the dirt.

After the fret wires are clean, you can clean the wood of the fretboard itself. A fretboard conditioner is highly recommended to keep your fretboard from wearing and cracking. Many cleaning kits will include a fretboard conditioner, or you can purchase one separately. In either case, follow the directions on the bottle of conditioner.

The body of the guitar can be cleaned with a clean microfiber or lint-free cloth. Using a guitar polish or wax can really make your instrument shine. Again, just like the conditioner, please read and follow the directions of whatever polish or wax you choose. A small amount can go a long way.

Restringing Your Guitar

This may seem a bit intimidating, but the only way to learn how to restring your guitar is by actually doing it. So take it slow, follow along carefully, and you'll master it in no time.

Tip 43: Before you restring your guitar, make sure you have the right tools for the job.

Obviously, you'll need replacement strings. Which string brand and gauge is mostly a personal choice. Just make sure you get acoustic guitar strings if you have an acoustic guitar and electric guitar strings for your electric guitar. The difference matters in how the strings are wound and the thickness of the strings. For beginners, the lighter the gauge, the easier on the fingers.

A string winder and a pair of wire clippers. Must-have tools for restringing.

You will also want a couple of tools. First is a string winder. This tool attaches to the tuning key and makes turning it a much faster process than using your hand. Winding a string around a tuning peg by hand is possible, but it takes a lot more time and effort. A string winder makes it fast and easy.

Next, you will need a pair of wire clippers. You will be using the wire clippers to help you remove the old strings and trim the new ones once they are properly wound. Any standard wire clippers will do.

If you are restringing an acoustic guitar, you will also need a bridge pin puller. The pins in the bridge of an acoustic guitar are usually made of plastic. You can pull these out with a pair of pliers, but you risk damaging or completely cracking them. So instead, a bridge pin puller slides underneath the bridge pin, allowing you to safely remove the bridge pin.

It is also recommended that you get a non-slip mat and a neck cradle. The non-slip mat will give you a safe surface to work on without risking the guitar falling off of your workstation. The neck cradle elevates your guitar for an easier angle to restring it. Place your guitar on a table or countertop to restring your guitar. Don't try to do it on a soft surface, like a bed or couch, or on your lap.

Tip 44: *The process for restringing your guitar can change slightly depending on what kind of tuning machines your guitar has.*

A standard tuning peg requires you to wind the string two to four times completely around it, and then the strings are trimmed. Vintage tuners need strings to be trimmed before winding them around the pegs. Locking tuners have an interior post that locks the string in place, eliminating the need to wind the strings around the peg at all.

Since most beginner guitars have standard tuning pegs, we will discuss that process.

Tip 45: *The first step in restringing your guitar is to remove the tension on all of the strings completely.*

There is some debate as to whether or not to remove all the tension from all of the strings or to do it one at a time to keep the neck of the guitar straight. As we have already discussed, removing all of the strings makes cleaning the fretboard much easier. So, for our purposes, we will unwind all of the strings.

Use the string winder to unwind all of the strings completely. You will turn the tuning peg in the direction that tunes the strings down, relieving the tension on the strings. Pull the strings out from the tuning pegs carefully. The ends of guitar strings can be very sharp. Then, cut the strings about six inches away from the bridge. Trimming them this way makes removing them from the bridge easier. Finally, wrap up and dispose of the excess strings.

Tip 46: The type of bridge will dictate how you remove the strings from the bridge. Pay attention to how you remove the strings because that's how you will put them back.

Acoustic guitars have bridge pins holding the strings in place. Use your bridge pin puller to pull the pins straight up and remove the strings from the hole. Dispose of the strings, but do not throw away the bridge pins.

If your electric guitar has a string-through design, push the strings through the bridge and pull them out of the back of the body. If your guitar has a hard- or stop-tail bridge, push the strings through the bridge and remove them. Throw away the strings.

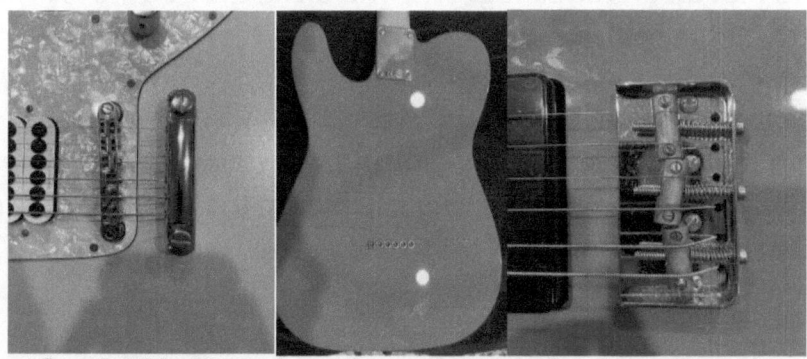

Left: A hardtail bridge where the strings are fed through the bottom of the tailpiece.
Center: A string through body where the strings are fed through the back of the guitar.
Right: A string-through bridge with round brass saddles.

Tip 47: Make sure you are using the correct string in the proper position. Start with the thickest (sixth) string and work your way, one string at a time, to the thinnest (first) string.

Each guitar string pack will have a guide to which string should be used in which position. Some have colored "ball" ends (the end that sits in the bridge) that differentiate between the different strings. Others will have each string in its own individual pack, and you can keep track that way.

Take a new string and place the ball end into the bridge for an acoustic guitar. At the same time, place the bridge pin on top of the ball end of that new string. Next, slightly press down on the bridge pin and pull up on the string. This will ensure the string is seated properly in the bridge.

On an electric guitar, thread the string through the bridge or through the body if it is a string-through design. In either case, pay attention to the groove the string sits into in the bridge. Make sure it is seated properly and not off to one side or the other of the groove.

After you have the string seated properly in the bridge, feed the string through the hole in the tuning peg. To make this easier, before you feed the string through, turn the tuning key so that the hole in the peg is in line with the neck of the guitar.

Tip 48: You have to create the right amount of slack in the string so that you can wind it around the tuning peg.

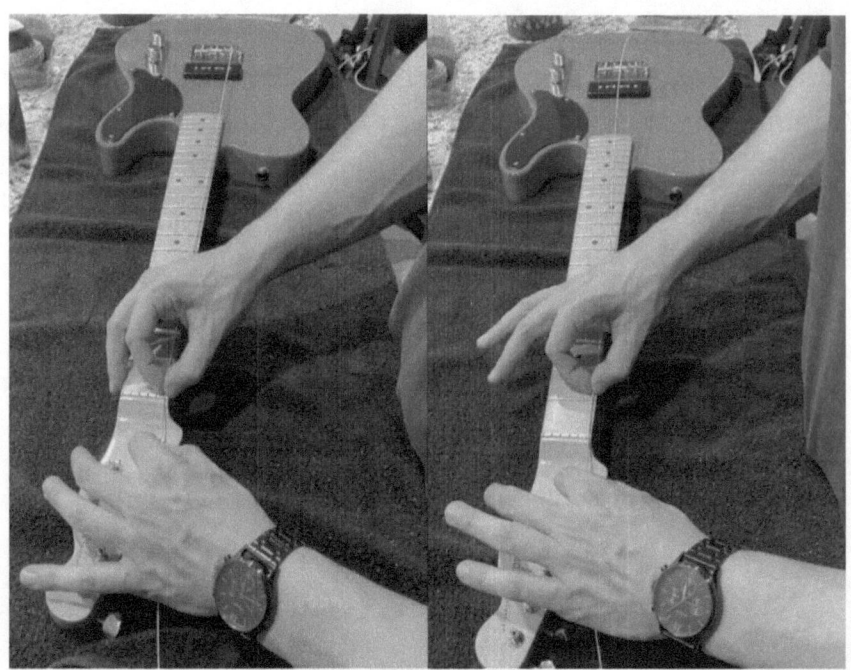

Left: pull the string tight. Right: pull it back one fret to create slack.
Notice the slack created near the bridge.

To begin, pull the string all the way through the peg. Next, hold the string slightly taut on the end farthest away from the body with one hand. Next, pinch the string at the nut and pull it back to the first fret with the other hand. Finally, use your first (pointer) finger to hold the string down on the fretboard at the guitar with that same hand. If done properly, you should create some slack in the guitar string to wind it around the peg.

Tip 49: When winding the string, keep it winding down in one direction.

That means you don't want the wraps around the tuning peg to overlap each other. To keep the string winding down as you tighten it, maintain pressure with your index finger. Make sure the loose end of the string travels over your finger and the string it is holding down. Keep it in a nice, neat downward spiral. Use your string winder to tighten the string.

Keep tension on the string while winding by using your index finger to push down near the peg and your other fingers holding up the slack.

Don't over-tighten the string. If you've left enough slack, 2 to 3 wraps of the string should be fine. Once you have the string wrapped around the peg, cut off the excess string but leave about ¼ of an inch (about 6mm) on the end. This is just for when the string stretches during tuning or regular playing.

Tip 50: Do not tune that string until you have restrung all six strings. Tune the guitar after you've done all six strings.

As you tighten the strings one at a time, you are creating tension on the neck. If you tune the sixth string before you restring the fifth, the sixth string will be completely out of tune by the time you put the new string on. So, restring the guitar completely before you tune it and follow the steps from the previous section.

When to See a Professional

Tip 51: Similar to a car, it's a good idea to take your guitar in to see a technician about once a year.

Experienced guitar technicians can do wonders on new guitars, especially during the first setup. But, once a year, you can take your guitar into your local guitar shop for a thorough setup. They will likely check the intonation, level or smooth out the frets, adjust the neck if necessary, and do other steps to make your guitar play phenomenally.

Obviously, if something is wrong with the guitar, like it won't stay in tune or if your electric guitar won't work when plugged in, take it into the shop. But, if you're not sure, give them a phone call first to see if it's something they can take care of for you.

Don't be afraid to ask questions, either. Guitar technicians, in general, enjoy sharing their knowledge with new musicians. Your local guitar shop can be a great place to learn about your instrument and the local music scene. Once you're feeling confident, you might even find a band that's looking for a guitarist.

Summary

- Store your guitar properly, either on a stand or in a case.
- The easiest way to tune your guitar is by purchasing a guitar tuner.
- Standard guitar tuning is E-A-D-G-B-E
- Use correct guitar cleaning solutions to clean your guitar, and don't use ordinary household cleaners.
- Take your time when restringing your guitar.
- Leave enough slack to wrap the string 2 to 3 times around the tuning peg when restringing.
- Make sure the string wraps around the tuning peg in a neat, downward wrap without any overlap.

Chapter 5: Holding Your Guitar

When presented with the option of choosing my own guitar, I was overwhelmed. Sure, I had flipped through guitar shopping catalogs. But I never really knew exactly what I wanted. They all looked cool!

So, when my dad gave me a budget to pick a guitar, I just went with what looked coolest (and within my price range)--a sharp, blue shred machine. It was the right size, fit well in my hands, and wasn't too heavy. Yup. This was the one for sure.

Until I got it home and plugged it in. I played for a few hours, adjusted the strap up and down, hoping that I would grow into the guitar. Or it would grow into me.

I made a mistake. The guitar I had picked was great... if you were looking to be a heavy metal shredding virtuoso. That wasn't what I wanted to be.

Punk rock was the music that spoke to me. Loud, fast, unapologetic, and far from technical. I needed a guitar that could withstand big strumming from the shoulder and a fat, chunky neck that I could grip onto like my life depended on it.

Except, I didn't know that at the time. I had picked the wrong guitar, and I was stuck with it.

I still loved playing guitar. So, I kept playing and practicing, even if the guitar I had in my hands wasn't the perfect guitar.

And that was okay. Because I also had my first part-time job. I saved every penny I could because the next guitar would be perfect.

You'll be playing your guitar one of two ways: sitting or standing. We'll go over both positions for both acoustic and electric guitars. However, when first learning either acoustic or electric guitar, you'll absolutely want to be sitting.

Sitting With Your Acoustic Guitar

Tip 52: Your acoustic guitar should fit comfortably on the same leg as your dominant hand. If you're right-handed, the guitar will be on your right leg, vice versa if you're left-handed.

You should be seated on a chair with no armrests, or ideally, on a stool. The chair shouldn't be too high or too low; your feet should be comfortably flat on the floor. If you are on a chair with a backrest, don't lean against it. Instead, sit near or on the edge of the seat.

Also, no slouching! Sit with your back straight. You'll probably have to remind yourself to sit straight a few times, as you might lean forward or over the guitar as you concentrate on playing.

Tip 53: The guitar should be right up against your body while seated.

Don't let it get so far away from you that you have to reach for it. Keeping it close will also keep the weight of the guitar on your leg, as opposed to having to hold it up with your hands.

The neck of the guitar should be somewhere near parallel to the floor. A slight angle upward is okay; just don't be pointing the headstock straight to the sky! The arm of your fretting hand should have a slight bend to it, keeping the elbow close to your body. The arm of your strumming hand will rest over the top of the body. Use the elbow of your strumming arm to keep the guitar close.

Sitting With Your Electric Guitar

Tip 54: No two electric guitars are the same; no, there is no "one size fits all" approach to sitting with an electric guitar.

Ideally, the body of your electric guitar will be ergonomic and "curvy." There will be a curve on one side of the body that lets it sit comfortably on your leg. Same as the acoustic guitar, the electric guitar will rest on the leg of your dominant side. If you have a uniquely shaped guitar, you might have to find another way to sit.

For example, a "V" shaped body guitar would slide right off your leg if you tried to hold it like an acoustic guitar. This is because a "V" shaped guitar is held mostly vertical, with the interior angle of the body resting on the dominant leg. This is for those gnarly guitar solos on the higher frets. You'll get there someday.

Like the acoustic guitar, the electric guitar will be held close to your body, the arm of the strumming hand over the body of the guitar, and the arm of the fretting hand slightly bent with the elbow pointing towards the body.

Tip 55: *If you're having difficulty strumming properly, try the "classical" seated position.*

Move the guitar over to the non-dominant leg, with the larger, bottom portion of the guitar in between your right and left legs. The guitar may be held slightly more vertical in this position, but you should still keep it close to your body.

Alternatively, you can cross one leg over the other, with your ankle resting on your thigh. The foot on the floor should still be flat on the floor. The guitar would rest on the leg that is crossed over the top of the other leg.

Again, being "comfortable" is a relative term. Holding your guitar will always feel awkward at first. Just try to find a position that is somewhat natural to you, allows you to keep your back straight, and doesn't cause any pain. Your strumming hand should always be somewhere in the middle of the body of the guitar, not over the neck or too close to the bridge.

Tip 56: *While seated with either an acoustic or electric guitar, it is good practice to still have the strap on the guitar and over your shoulder.*

Although the guitar will still be mostly supported by the leg it is rested on, having the guitar strap on properly adds a little extra "insurance" should your guitar slip off of your leg. So make sure the strap is on properly. You might also want to shorten the length of the strap, as well, just to make sure the guitar doesn't fall all the way to the floor if it still slips off.

Standing With Your Acoustic Guitar

Tip 57: You will always need a guitar strap when standing with either an acoustic or an electric guitar.

Make sure your acoustic guitar has at least one "strap button" located at the bottom of the body. In addition, some acoustic guitars will have another strap button located on the back of the body, near the neck joint where the neck meets the body. Figure out how many strap buttons your acoustic guitar has before buying a strap.

If your acoustic guitar only has one strap button, you will need a guitar strap that has a lace or string on one end. At that end, you will tie around the headstock, above the nut, and under the strings. Be sure to search specifically for "acoustic guitar straps" when looking for these kinds of straps online. If your guitar has two strap buttons, then almost any strap will work.

Tip 58: Whichever strap you end up purchasing, it must be adjustable.

Everybody is different; no one is the same height or stature. So you'll more than likely need to adjust the height of your guitar by changing the length of the guitar strap. Start with the guitar high up and adjust it down until it's at the right height.

Tip 59: When standing, the acoustic guitar should generally be at the same height as when you are seated.

The same principles apply to your arms: strumming arm over the body, keeping the guitar close, fretting arm slightly bent with elbow tucked towards the body. Make sure you're standing nice and tall. Slouching while standing with a guitar strapped to your shoulder can hurt your back. Don't let that happen.

Standing With Your Electric Guitar

Tip 60: Standing while playing an electric guitar will also require a strap.

Every electric guitar will have two strap buttons. However, the positions of the buttons will vary from model to model. Some will have a button on the back of the body near the neck joint, similar to an acoustic guitar. Others will have the strap button located on the top "corner" of the body. The strap buttons should be pretty easy to locate.

The kind of strap you want is entirely up to you. There are plenty of straps to choose from with many different materials, from faux leather to cotton to nylon. Just make sure it's adjustable, the same as with an acoustic guitar strap.

Tip 61: Although not required, a strap lock system is highly recommended to avoid dropping your guitar.

Accidents happen, and guitar straps sometimes will slip off of strap buttons (believe me, I know). There are many systems available that will swap out the standard strap buttons to allow the strap to lock onto the guitar. Most of these are pretty easy to install and only require a screwdriver. Do a little research and see if you want to secure your guitar a little better with a strap lock system.

Tip 62: It might look cool, but having the guitar strap adjusted, so the guitar is super low is NOT the correct form.

When standing with an electric guitar, it should not be down below your belt line. If your strumming arm has to extend fully to reach all of the strings, your guitar is simply too low. This can cause strain and/or injury to your arm, wrist, or shoulder.

Left: the proper way to hold an electric guitar standing. Right: the incorrect way, which can cause wrist, shoulder, and back pain.

The electric guitar should be hung from a height that is similar to where the guitar is positioned when you are sitting down. See a pattern here? This form allows both of your arms to stay relaxed and retain a full range of motion, no matter what style of music you're playing. Also, keeping the guitar closer to your center of gravity can prevent unnecessary back strain.

Strumming Hand

You probably by now have noticed that we've referred to "fretting" hand and "strumming" hand as opposed to "left" and "right." Well, there's a good reason for that:

Tip 63: Your strumming hand is your dominant hand.

If you are right-handed, like 90% of the population, your strumming hand will be your right hand. However, some people are left-handed, so their strumming hand will be their left hand.

It almost seems backward, doesn't it? Playing notes on the fretboard seems complicated, so shouldn't the dominant hand be the fretting hand? But there are good reasons for the dominant hand to be the strumming hand.

The dominant hand is dominant for a reason; it does most of the work on a day-to-day basis. Believe it or not, the strumming hand on a guitar is doing more work than the fretting hand. It's keeping time and rhythm. You'll be learning upstrokes and downstrokes with the strumming hand.

There are finer movements involved when plucking individual strings, and the dominant hand excels at those fine motor skills. Also, the strumming hand is responsible for holding the guitar pick.

***Tip 64:** To properly hold a guitar pick, first make a fist. Then, move your thumb to the side of your fist. The guitar pick will slide in between your thumb and the side of your index finger. Finally, relax your middle, ring, and pinky fingers.*

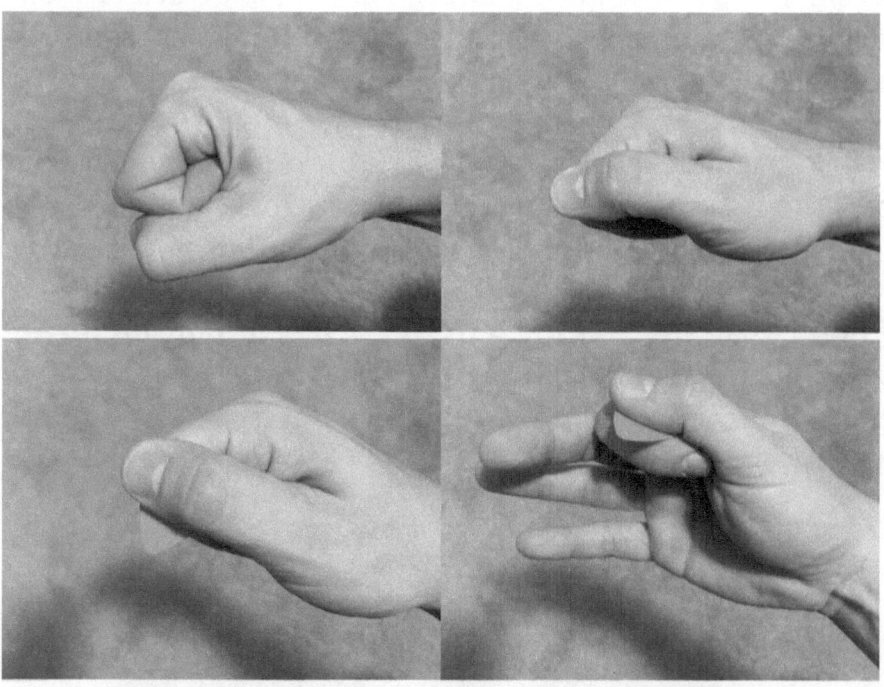

Learning to hold a guitar pick properly is vital when you first start playing guitar. So many people hold the pick incorrectly, which makes learning other techniques much harder down the road. Do yourself a favor from the start and hold the pick correctly. This is the proper grip for both acoustic and electric guitars.

In addition, don't grip the pick with a death grip. If you hold it too hard, your strumming arm won't move properly. It needs to be relaxed. Too light, and you will drop it. Find a happy medium. The pick should have some flex as you strum up and down the strings. Keeping your middle, ring, and pinky fingers relaxed will help you maintain a proper amount of grip pressure.

Finding the right thickness of your guitar pick is also vital. Guitar picks are available in a multitude of shapes, thicknesses, and materials. As with so many other things, the choice of your guitar pick ultimately comes down to personal preference. Thicker picks are more durable, more rigid, and better suited for lead guitar style playing. On the other hand, thinner picks are more flexible, less likely to break guitar strings, and are better suited for rhythm-style guitar playing.

Every local guitar shop will have guitar picks of various shapes and sizes. They're usually relatively cheap, as well. So grab a few of varying thicknesses and try them all out to see which best suits you.

Tip 65: Mute the strings with your fretting hand by lightly laying your fingers across the strings on the neck. Strum up and down a few times to get a feel on how to strum.

Strum from your elbow with the wrist relaxed.

Keep your wrist relaxed. Your elbow will be the pivot point, and it will assist in keeping your strumming hand moving. Don't hit the strings too hard. Listen to and feel the pick "click" against all six strings as you strum all the way up and down. All you want to hear is the clicking noise of the pick across the strings. If you hear any actual notes, you are pressing down with your fretting hand too hard.

First, practice a simple "one and two" pattern. Use a metronome (search on the internet "online metronome" for an easy and free one to use) set at a low tempo, like 70-80 beats per minute. Swing your arm up and down to keep the downswing on the beat. But only strum the strings on the downswing. On the "one" and "two" (on the beat), you'll hit the strings on the downstroke. On the "and" (in between the beats), your arm will be swinging up, but you won't make contact with the strings. Here's a table that might help you understand.

Where you see an "X" in the "Hit" box, strum the strings with the pick. Where there is no "X," keep moving your arm but don't strum the strings. Repeat the pattern with another "AND" at the end, and keep practicing until you've got it down.

Count:	ONE	AND	TWO	AND	ONE	AND	TWO
Strum:	DOWN	UP	DOWN	UP	DOWN	UP	DOWN
Hit:	X		X		X		X

Once you master that, you can move on to the next strumming pattern, which includes the "three and four" into the rhythm. You'll strum the same as the first pattern, only hitting the strings on the "one" and "two" going down, moving your arm up on the "and." On the "three and four," you will make contact with the strings on both the up and the down. It'll be something like this:

Count:	ONE	AND	TWO	AND	THREE	AND	FOUR
Strum:	DOWN	UP	DOWN	UP	DOWN	UP	DOWN
Hit:	X		X		X	X	X

Keep the tempo low and practice this rhythm. Say the count, "one and two and three and four" out loud while you practice. Most popular music is based on the four-count. Rhythm is nothing more than choosing on which beat to play the notes, or in our case, when to hit the strings. We'll get more into precise picking and playing individual notes in Chapter 8, "Scales."

Fretting Hand

Tip 66: Your fretting hand will be your non-dominant hand. For right-handers, that means your left hand will be on the neck. For left-handers, it will be your right.

If you're worried about playing notes with your "off" hand, don't be. It's awkward for everyone at first. But, over time, and with lots of practice, you will build up the dexterity and strength necessary to play guitar.

Tip 67: The fingers on your fretting hand will be numbered, one through four.

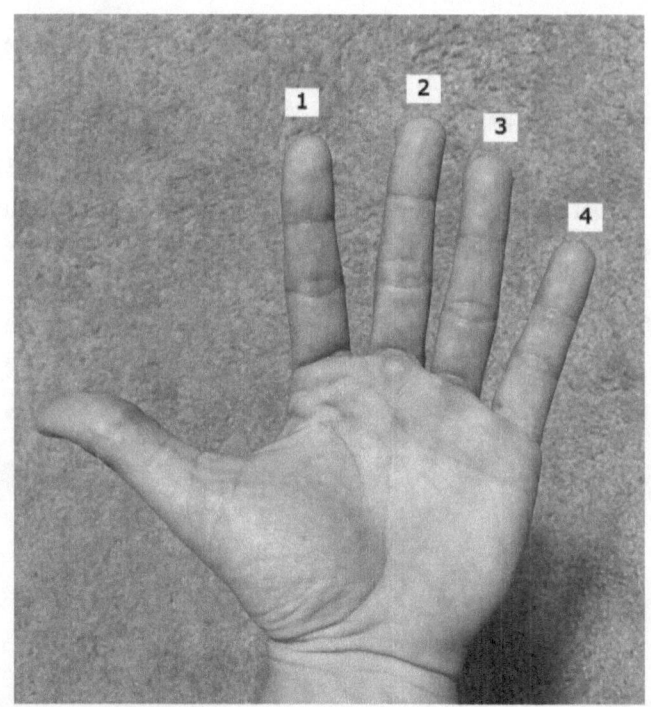

Numbered fingers. This is important to remember.

For ease of learning and teaching, the fingers on the fretting hand are referred to by numbers. Your index (pointer) finger will be number 1. Your middle finger will be number 2. Your ring finger will be number 3. And your pinky (little) finger will be number 4. Your thumb won't be playing any notes, so it doesn't get a number. Your thumb will be on the back of the neck, creating counter-pressure for your other fingers.

Tip 68: It is very important that you only use the very tips of your fingers to press down on the strings.

If you try to use the "pad" of your finger, you'll create a bend in your finger that blocks the adjacent strings. It will be difficult, at first, to press down hard enough on the strings to play notes. It takes time to build strength on your fingers. So here is a quick finger-strengthening exercise you can do: the 1, 2, 3, 4 drill.

Very simple, you will use your first finger on the first fret. You press down in the middle of the fret, not on top of the fret wire. Pluck the string with your strumming hand. Then, use your second finger to press down the second fret. Do not keep pressing the first fret. Play the note. The third finger on the third fret, and finally the fourth finger on the fourth. Easy as 1, 2, 3, 4!

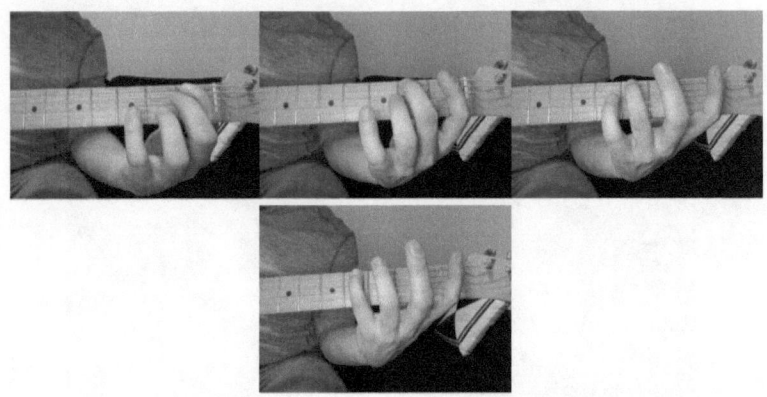

From left to right: The 1, 2, 3, 4 drill.

Take your time. Make sure you use just the tips of your fingers. Each note should ring true. If the note isn't clear or doesn't sound right, try pressing a little bit harder. Pressing too hard might make the note "sharp" or go up in pitch. Once you are able to play the notes consistently, use a metronome to maintain a steady pace and slowly increase it over time, still playing the notes properly.

There are a few variations you can do with this finger exercise. First, walk backward with your fingers the same as you did going up. 1, 2, 3, 4, 3, 2, and 1.

You can also walk up each individual string one at a time. So you'll play 1 through 4 on the sixth (bottom, thickest) string, then move on to the fifth and play 1 through 4, then to the fourth string, and so on for all six strings. This is also a great pick control exercise for your strumming hand.

Summary

- Acoustic and electric guitars can be played both while seated and while standing.
- While seated, the guitar goes on the leg on the same side of your dominant hand (left leg for left-handers, right leg for right-handers). The guitar stays close to your body, keeping your dominant arm relaxed and over the middle of the body.
- While standing, you will need a strap for either acoustic or electric. Adjust the strap so that the guitar is in mostly the same position as when you're seated.
- Your dominant hand is your strumming hand, responsible for keeping time and rhythm while also maintaining pick control.
- Practice keeping rhythm using the "one and two" and the "one and two and three and four" counts.
- Your non-dominant hand is your fretting hand on the neck and using your fingertips to press down on the frets.
- Strengthen your fretting hand fingers by playing notes one at a time with each individual finger (1, 2, 3, and 4).

Chapter 6: Basic Chords

In my hometown, there is a park that is right on the river. The sun sets on the water and makes the park look like a postcard. Local musicians would gather at this park every Thursday night to hang out and jam.

The country and bluegrass players would be under the gazebo. The blues musicians sat near the fountain. And the snot-nosed punk rock skateboarding teenagers would be at the picnic benches nearest the playground.

Guess where I would be.

On one fateful Thursday evening, I was with my bratty brethren, goofing around as teenagers do. I was feeling pretty confident with my guitar skills at this point, so I had brought my acoustic guitar along.

A friend of mine had picked it up and strummed a few chords when this guy carrying his own acoustic guitar approached our group.

He went to my friend and asked if he played. He replied, "Not really. This is his guitar," and pointed in my direction. So I came over and introduced myself.

He said his name was Chuck. Then, he asked what kind of music I listened to. We quickly bonded over similar musical tastes of the pop-punk and punk rock variety.

He said he was looking for a second guitarist and vocalist for his band and asked if I was interested.

I was very interested.

Now that we understand how to hold the guitar and strum it, we'll begin by playing a few basic chords. Simply put, a chord is a collection of notes that sound good when played all together.

The basic chords taught in this chapter can be found in most popular music today and are used in virtually every genre. Once you understand and can play these chords, an entire catalog of songs will be opened up to you.

Tip 69: The first thing you'll need to understand is that musical notes are listed by the letters of the alphabet, "A" through "G."

It is important to know this now because the basic chords are referred to by their corresponding musical note. Later on in this book, you'll learn where these notes lie and how to fully understand and incorporate these notes into your guitar playing in the chapter dedicated to scales.

It is also important to remember that your fingers are numbered one through four, one being your index finger, and four is your pinky. You will see these numbers on the following chord charts.

Chord Charts

Tip 70: Chord charts are an easy way to see, at a glance, how to play a specific chord.

A chord chart looks like a box with lines and squares. Each vertical line represents a string on the guitar; the sixth (thickest) string is on the left, and the first (thinnest) is on the right. Each box represents a fret on the neck. A black dot inside a box is a finger holding down the string at that particular fret. It's like a straight-on view of the neck of the guitar.

If you trace the line down from the dot, there will be a number showing you which finger should hold down that fret. At the top of the chart, a circle will represent a string that is played "open" (without any fingers holding it down). An "X" represents a string that is not played or blocked with an adjacent finger.

G Chord

This leads us to the first chord you will learn: the G chord.

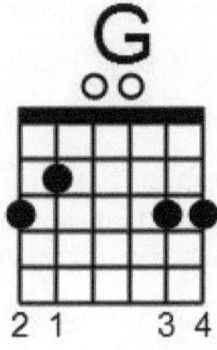

Tip 71: *Take a look at the chord chart. The G chord is played with the second finger on the sixth string, the first finger on the fifth. The fourth and third strings are played open. The third finger holds down the second string, and the fourth finger holds down the first string.*

G chord

Strum the chord and listen to each string. You should clearly hear each note on each string. If something sounds "off," hold the chord and pluck each string individually. If the sixth, fifth, second, or first string doesn't sound right, make sure you're pressing down firmly with each finger. If the fourth or third strings aren't ringing clearly, make sure you're using the tips of your fingers and that your fingers aren't blocking the open strings.

There's a very good reason to first learn the G chord. First, it utilizes all six strings of the guitar and all four fingers of your fretting hand. Because of this, it allows you to pay attention to how your fretting hand works on the guitar, making sure each note is played correctly.

Second, the fingers of the fretting hand are in a relatively comfortable position. They're not overcrowded or stretching or crossing over each other. With the G chord, you can hold your fretting fingers down and strengthen your fingertips.

Third, the G chord is widely used in popular music. From country to rock to pop, you'll find the G chord scattered all over the place! Once you develop a musical ear, you'll be able to spot a G chord from a mile away.

E Chord

The next chord we will learn is the E chord. Here is the chord chart:

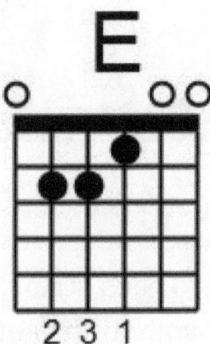

Tip 72: The E chord only utilizes the first, second, and third fingers. The first finger is on the first fret of the fourth string. The second and third fingers are on the second fret of the fifth and fourth strings. The rest of the strings are played open.

E chord. Notice the thumb is away from the sixth string.

The E chord can be a little trickier because the fingers are now closer together. Your fretting hand might be uncomfortable holding this chord for too long, at least at first. Give yourself time and practice to build up strength in the hand and calluses on the fingertips.

Just like the G chord, the E chord incorporates the open strings. Only this time, the open strings are the sixth, second, and first. The challenge with the E chord is not to let your thumb or the fingers block those open strings.

Tip 73: *For all chords, make sure you use only the tips of your fingers. Your thumb can rest on the back of the neck or near the top. Don't let your thumb block the sixth string.*

This becomes especially important on the E chord and the rest of the chords moving forward. Beginners can sometimes press down too hard, causing their fingers to flatten too much. If the pad of your finger (where your fingerprint is) is pressing down on the string, you'll block the other strings, preventing notes from playing when they should.

If you are having trouble only using your fingertips, make sure to use the "1-2-3-4" exercise: one finger at a time, play the first finger on the first fret, then play the second finger on the second fret, the third finger on the third fret, fourth finger on the fourth fret, and go back down. Again, use only your fingertips and make sure the notes ring true.

D Chord

Now, we will move the fingers a little closer together in the D chord. The chord chart looks like this:

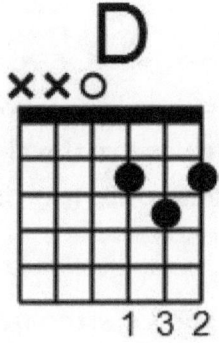

Tip 74: For the D chord, the first finger is on the second fret of the third string. The third finger is on the third fret of the second string. The second finger is on the second fret of the first string. The only open string played is the fourth string.

D chord. Now, the thumb is blocking the sixth string intentionally.

You might find your fingers a bit twisted for this one. It may appear to be complicated or taxing. However, in actuality, the fretting fingers are again in a more natural position. Some might find it easier to play than the G chord!

Also, notice the "X's" above the sixth and fifth strings. That means that those two strings are not played in this chord. You have two options. You can just strum strings four through one. Or you can wrap your thumb around and lightly lay it on top of the sixth string.

Bringing your thumb around to block the sixth string is perfectly acceptable in this case. In fact, it can be a useful skill going forward. As you progress and begin to utilize full strumming, you will want to use your thumb to block strings that you don't want to play during certain chords. More on that later. For now, let's move on.

C Chord

Here is the chord chart for the C chord:

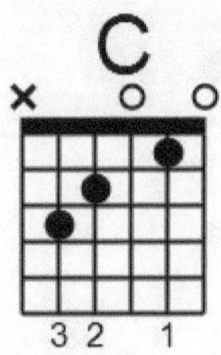

Tip 75: *The sixth string is either blocked with the thumb or not played. The third finger holds the third fret on the fifth string. The second finger is on the second fret on the fourth string; the third string is open. The first finger is on the first fret of the second string. The first string is played open.*

C chord. Again, the thumb is blocking the sixth string.

The C chord can be another tricky chord for some. It involves some stretching between the first and second fingers. Again, using only the fingertips is crucial here. Be sure you're not blocking the third and first open strings.

Here again, we have a blocked string. This time, it's only the sixth string. As before, you can simply not strum the sixth string, or you can use your thumb to mute that string when full strumming.

A Chord

Finally, here is the chord chart for the A chord:

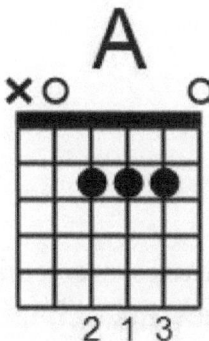

Tip 76: The A chord is only played on strings five through one, similar to the C chord. The fifth and first strings are open. Fingers one through three are all on the second fret. Finger two is on the fourth string, finger one on the third, and finger three on the second.

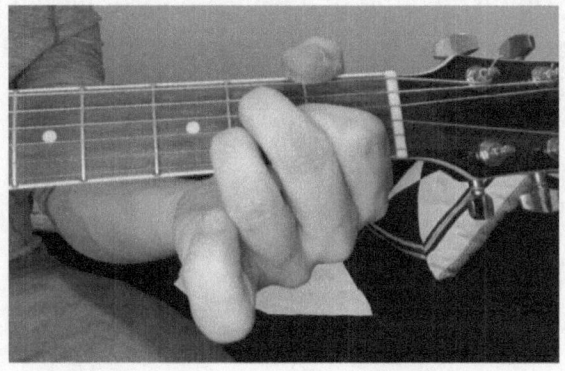

A chord

You may find this similar to the E chord we learned earlier. Essentially, it is the same chord as the E. All of the notes are spaced the same as the E chord. The difference is that the "root" note is the open A string as opposed to the open E string of the E chord.

If you are having difficulty with the finger position of the A chord, you can use your fingers in order. First finger on the fourth string, the second finger on the third string, and the third finger on the second string.

Major vs. Minor

All of the chords we just learned were "major" chords. These are chords that sound bright, cheerful, or happy. They can be uplifting, and songwriters use them to write songs that evoke those emotions in the listener.

Conversely, chords that sound sad, down, or melancholy are called "minor" chords. It's important to know these chords. The juxtaposition between the major and minor chords creates drama and tension in a song. The "up" feeling of a major chord can be followed by a "down" feeling of a minor chord, which is then followed by another "up" to bring the listener back. Music is just a roller coaster of emotions!

We'll see how simply changing one note can change the entire "feel" of a chord with our first minor chord.

Am Chord

Take a look at the chord chart for the A minor chord (note that minor chords are indicated by the lowercase "m"):

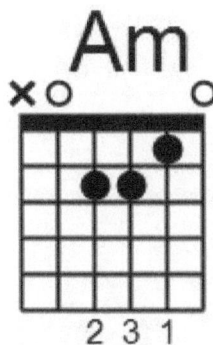

Tip 77: The Am chord is similar to the A chord. The strings played are the same. However, the finger positioning is a little different. The first finger is moved to the first fret on the second string. The second finger is on the second fret of the fourth string. The third finger is on the second fret on the third string.

A minor chord

If you play this chord correctly, you should be able to hear the difference between the A major chord and the A minor chord. It sounds like a completely different chord, even though only one note has changed!

Em Chord

The E minor chord makes the same change to the E major chord. Here is the chart:

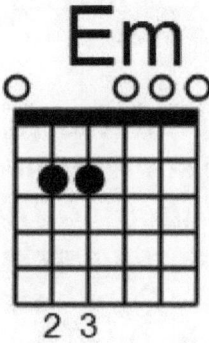

Tip 78: If you look back to the E major chord chart, you'll see that the E minor is virtually the same. Except for the minor chord, you remove the first finger from the fourth string.

E minor chord

Once again, changing one note makes all the difference in the world! Play the E major and the E minor back-to-back a few times to really appreciate the tonal differences between major and minor chords.

Dm Chord

Finally, here is the chord chart for the D minor chord:

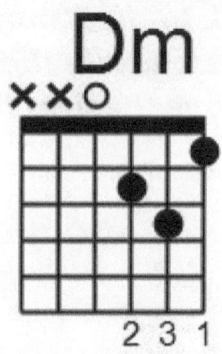

***Tip 79:** The sixth and fifth strings are still muted or not played. The fourth string is played open. The second finger is on the second fret of the third string. The third finger is on the third fret of the second string, and the first finger is on the first fret of the first string.*

Although we are still only making the one-note change from major to minor, the finger positioning for the D minor chord is very different from the D major chord.

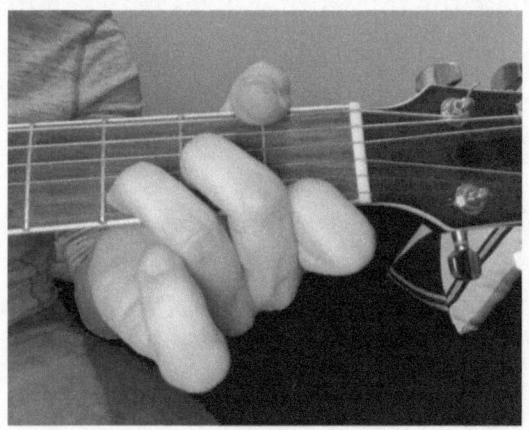

D minor chord

The D minor chord may be a little bit more comfortable to play than its big brother, the D major chord. This is because the fingers are not bunched as closely together and rest in a more natural position.

Again, keep an ear out for the difference between the major and minor chords. One should sound happy and hopeful. The other should sound sad and gloomy.

Tip 80: Before moving on, make sure you have mastered and are relatively comfortable playing all of these chords.

You have to crawl before you can walk. Take your time with all of these chords. Get them down pat without having to look at the chord charts. Strum them all slowly to make sure you're playing each note clearly. Use both downstrokes and upstrokes when playing them. The more comfortable you are with these chords, the easier the next steps will be.

Chord Progressions

Are you ready to put one foot in front of the other? Then, we're going to switch between chords, string them together, and play something that might sound like a song!

Tip 81: Moving from one chord to another can be a very difficult process to learn. The most important thing is first to take it slow.

Other guitar books or lessons might have you practice these progressions along with a metronome. While that might come in handy down the line, it's easier at first to go at your own pace and rhythm.

All of these chord progressions will use only major chords. They will all be following the I-IV-V pattern. If you've forgotten your Roman numerals, that means "one, four, and five." Again, remember that musical notes are marked as A through G. Now, think of the letters as being numbered one through seven. A is I, B is II, C is III, and so forth. The first chord progression will start with the A major chord:

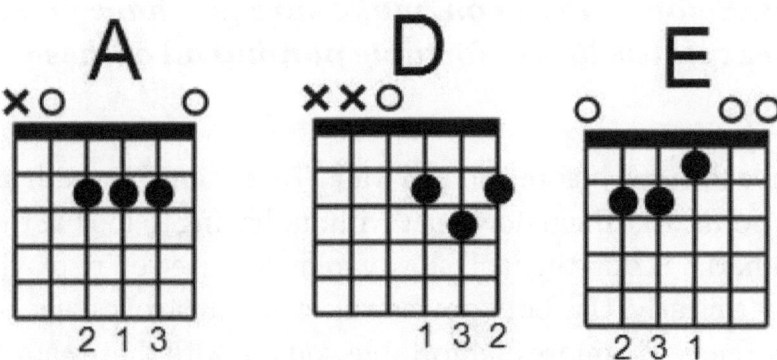

Strum the A chord four times using only downstrokes. Then, move your fingers to the D chord. Strum it four times. Lastly, make the E chord and strum four more times. Then, go back to the A chord and repeat.

Remember to take your time and not rush. The transition between chords must be as smooth as possible. Once they are smooth, you can speed it up just a bit. When practicing, always start slow to make your movements smooth. Once smooth, your movements will become faster.

Tip 82: *The chord progression I-IV-V is always the same. The first chord changes, and the other two adjust accordingly.*

Now, we will start with the D chord. If the D chord becomes our "I," then alphabetically, our "IV" becomes the G chord. Since there is no note after G, we got back around to the beginning of our musical alphabet. The A chord becomes our "V." The I-IV-V progression for the D chord is:

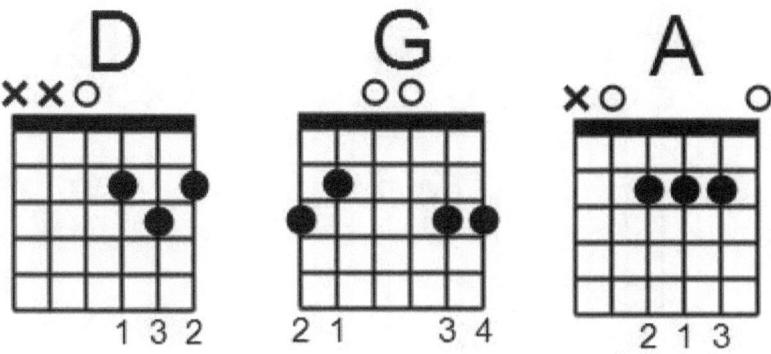

Same as before. Strum the D chord four times, change to the G, strum four times, change to the A, strum four times, and repeat.

To bring our minor chords into a chord progression, they are marked with lowercase Roman numerals. For example, our first minor chord progression will be "ii-V-I." It starts with a minor chord and finishes with two major chords. If the "I" is a C chord, can you figure out what the other two chords would be?

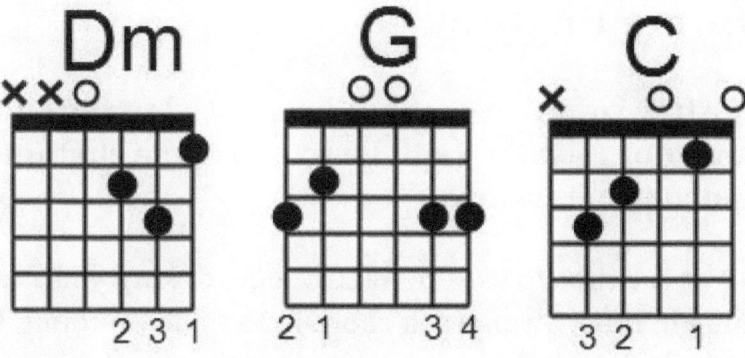

If you'll notice between the Dm chord and the G chord, your third finger stays in the same position: on the third fret of the second string. So you don't have to lift your finger between these two chords. Obviously, that all changes once you get to the C chord. But it's a neat little trick to watch out for in the next chord progression. We'll use the D chord as our "I":

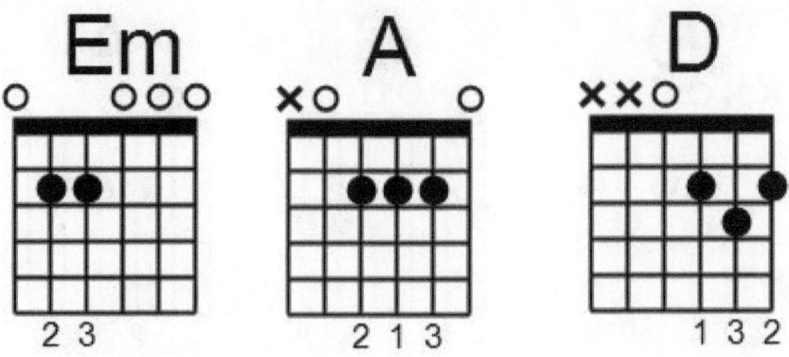

By this point, the transitions between these three chords should be relatively simple. Most of the fretting stays on the second fret. There are plenty of open strings to play, and your hand moves naturally from the low end of the strings to the high end. Just like before, strum each chord four times before moving to the next, and repeat after the final chord.

Add Some Rhythm

Tip 83: After your fretting hand gets used to the chord changes, your next step will be to add some rhythm to your chord progressions.

Now will be the time to use that metronome to keep your strumming in time. Strum each chord for a full four-count. Use the rhythms from the previous chapter to play the chord progressions. Start slow, make it smooth, and then speed it up only after you've gotten it smooth.

This is Not the End

Tip 84: By no means are these the "be-all-end-all" chords and chord progressions.

These first few chords are only meant to be an introduction to basic major and minor chords. They are also the most universal and commonly-known chords.

There are a near-infinite number of chords and chord variations to discover. On top of that, chords can be mixed and matched into whatever progression your heart and your ears desire.

Research and discover for yourself! Keep a careful ear out to whatever music you are listening to. Figure out what chords are being used, in what order, and how often. Try to decipher the rhythms.

Of course, this also doesn't take into account alternate tunings or using a capo. Overwhelming? Sure. Exciting? Absolutely.

Summary

- A chord chart is a quick way to see how a chord is played. It uses lines and boxes to represent strings and frets, similar to a frontal view of the guitar's fretboard.
- Musical notes are listed A through G. Chords correspond to and are named after these musical notes.
- Practice and master the five basic major chords: G, E, D, C, and A.
- Understand the minor chords, how they sound, and how to play them: Am, Em, and Dm.

- Chord progressions use Roman numerals to indicate which chord to play. Lowercase lettered Roman numerals are minor chords.
- Take it slow, make it smooth, and speed it up only after it's smooth.

Chapter 7: Scales

Despite not lasting more than three months playing trumpet back in fifth grade, I always had a lean towards the musical side.

Throughout middle school, I was in chorus class (6th, 7th, and 8th grades). The teacher of the class was a kind, older woman whose passion for singing and music filled the oversized chorus room. I met some of my best friends in that class. We would even meet in the chorus room before our first class to hang out with each other and the chorus teacher.

In that chorus class, I discovered a love for harmony and melody. There was always something intriguing to me about how voices could overlap and interweave and create a whole new sound, the sum greater than its parts. My middle school chorus teacher passionately taught us how to recognize and apply harmony and melody.

Looking back at those lessons, I now realize how complicated those concepts truly are. Yet, I was very fortunate to have that chorus teacher. She was able to engage, entertain, and educate seamlessly.

The lessons learned in those classes carried over quite well when I started playing in my first real band.

A scale is an ordered arrangement of notes that are played in ascending or descending order in a particular key. If you've ever taken singing lessons, you might remember your "Do-Re-Mi-Fa-So-La-Ti-Do" scale.

To some, scales can be the most intimidating part of learning an instrument. It can also be the most tedious. However, to truly master any instrument, you must fully embrace and understand the meaning and beauty of scales.

Tip 85: *If music is a language, musical notes are the letters. Scales are how to turn those letters into words and phrases.*

We already understand from our basic chords that musical notes are listed as letters in the alphabet, "A" through "G." Scales will show you which notes to play in certain scenarios. For example, if a song is in the key of C major, you will use the notes contained within the C major scale.

We'll begin by playing individual notes.

One Note at a Time

There are many additional benefits to learning scales and playing one note at a time. First, you will increase your finger dexterity and strength on your fretting hand. Your strumming hand will also develop finer movement patterns, and you'll play with more accuracy. Finally, learning your scales can also help you develop a more musical ear. You'll be able to pick out the notes that make up a beautiful harmony.

Tip 86: It may help you play individual notes to "anchor" your strumming hand pinky to the body of the guitar.

Anchoring the strumming hand by resting the pinky on the body of the guitar.

Simply by resting the pinky of your strumming hand, you may feel more stable and secure when playing individual notes. Of course, as with all things guitar, one size or technique may not work for everyone. But, to start, it may help you when you first begin playing one string at a time.

You might also rest your wrist or upper arm on the body of the guitar. If you're playing an acoustic guitar and you have the right size, your strumming arm should still be resting comfortably on the top of the body, just like when you were strumming your chords.

Remember how to properly hold the guitar pick: in between the pad of your thumb and the side of your index finger. Firm enough to keep it stable, but not too firm where your hand is totally tense.

When picking one note and one string at a time, try to think about pressing down with your thumb and following through with your wrist. The movement should be relatively small to avoid any string you don't want to play.

Pay attention to how hard or how soft you hit the string and how that "attack" changes the sound of the string being played.

Tip 87: *When first playing individual notes and strings, only worry about playing the notes with a downstroke of the guitar pick.*

Just like playing chords, individual notes can be played with upstrokes and downstrokes. There are many different techniques when playing individual notes rapidly. But remember how we learned our chords. Slow and smooth at first. Speed comes later.

If you haven't already practiced the "1-2-3-4" drill, now would be the time to do so. Not only should you practice this drill, but you should also have it nearly mastered. All four fingers should be equally as strong and ready to play. Because when we start playing our scales, we will be using all four fingers.

C Major Scale (open)

The first scale we'll learn is the C Major scale in the open position. The open position means we'll be playing on the lower frets (one through four) and utilizing the open strings. So, your fretting hand will generally be in the same position as the chords learned in the previous chapter.

Tip 88: Recall back to the C major chord you learned in Chapter 6. The C Major scale starts with the third fret on the fifth string.

That note is the root note of the chord and the first note of the scale, "C." You'll play that note with the same finger as you did with the chord: the third finger. Also, note that the third finger is playing the third fret. For the open position, all of your fretting hand fingers will correspond with the fret you will play, i.e., the first finger on the first fret, second finger on the second fret, etc.

Play just the fifth string while holding down the third fret of the fifth string. Then play the fourth string open without holding down any frets; that is a "D" note. Next, your second finger presses down on the second fret of the fourth string, just like in the C chord. That note is an "E." The next note is played on the fourth string as well. Next, your third finger holds down the third fret to play the "F" note. The next note is the "G" note of the open third string. So, play the third string open. Now, press down on the second fret of the third string and play that note. You're now playing the "A" note. Next, play the open second string for the "B" note. Finally, your first finger holds down the first fret of the second string. Play that note, and you've made it all the way back around to the higher octave "C" note.

Here is a scale chart for the C major scale:

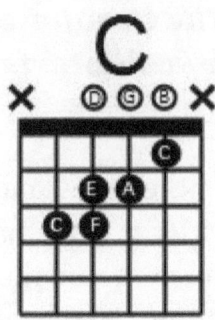

Notice that the scale chart for C Major looks very similar to the chord chart of the C chord. Except for this time, we're looking at the individual notes played. Start with the "C" on the fifth string and play in alphabetical order all the way to the "C" on the second string.

Take your time. Play the notes properly so that they all ring true. Then, repeat this scale until you can play it without referring back to the chart.

Tip 89: Scales can be extended in either direction, from the open sixth "E" string to as high on the fretboard you can go.

So, we'll continue to expand our C Major scale. First, we'll work our way down from the root note "C" on the fifth string. Then, play the "B" note on the fifth string by pressing the second fret with your second finger. Next, the "A" note is played on the open fifth string. Moving over to the sixth string, play the "G" note on the third fret with your third finger. Then, your first finger presses on the first fret of the sixth string, and you can play the "F" note. Finally, the open "E" string is the lowest note we can play on guitar in the C Major scale.

Now, we can work our way up the scale. We'll start on the high "C" played with the first finger on the first fret of the second string. Then, you will play the third fret of the second string to play a "D" note. Next, play the open first string for the "E" note. Followed by the first finger on the first fret; that's an "F" note. Finally, your third finger on the third fret of the first string is a "G" note.

The entire chord chart for C Major scale in open position looks like this:

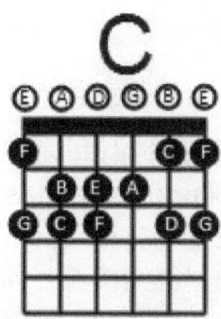

A few things to note in the C Major scale: First, recognize that all of the open strings are utilized in the C Major scale. Second, only "whole" notes are used. There are no sharp or flat notes. We'll get into those in another section. Third, since there are only whole notes, it makes it easier to learn as a beginner. Finally, we only use fingers one through three to play the entire scale.

Tip 90: It may help to think of scales (and scale charts) as a road map.

As long as you're in the key of C Major and you stay with these notes on this scale, you won't get lost. Much like finding your way around town, it gets easier if you just memorize the directions. This is why practice is essential when learning your scales. It may be tedious but keep playing this scale over and over again. Start all the way at the bottom on the low "E" note and work your way all the way up to the highest "G" note in the C Major scale.

A Minor Pentatonic

Do not be intimidated by the fancy words! This scale is quintessential when first learning how to play. The scale, or rather its shape (more on that in a bit), is used in nearly every genre of music. Once you master this scale, a whole new world of playing is opened up to you!

This scale starts on the fifth fret of the sixth string. You will use your first finger to play this note, which is an "A." This is the root, or tonic, note. Remember that. It is very important. Then, you will use your fourth finger on the eighth fret on the same string.

Tip 91: When using your fourth finger to press down a fret, you will have to bend your wrist and press your thumb on the back of the neck to create counter-pressure.

If you haven't already discovered, the fourth finger tends to be the weakest finger on the fretting hand. Anatomy dictates that you'll have to use more muscles than just those in your little finger to create enough pressure to play the note correctly. So, make sure you utilize your thumb on the back of the neck of the guitar to squeeze on the fretboard.

After these first two notes, you will move on to the fifth string. Your first finger will play the fifth fret on the fifth string. Then, the third finger will play the seventh fret on the same string. Next, the first finger moves over to the fifth fret on the fourth string. Finally, the third finger will go to the seventh fret again, this time on the fourth string.

Move on to the third string. Again, the first finger plays the fifth fret, and the third finger plays the seventh fret. Then, on to the second string, the first finger plays the fifth fret, and the fourth finger plays the eighth fret. Finally, the first finger plays the fifth fret on the first string, and the fourth finger plays the eighth fret again.

The A Minor Pentatonic scale chart is this:

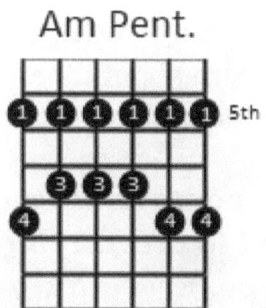

A few more important things to note here, as well: The first thing has to do with the first finger. Notice that it is always playing the fifth fret of every string. Second, notice that instead of showing you which notes are being played, this chart shows which finger you are playing. Because the important thing to remember is not the notes but the shape of the frets being played.

Tip 92: *The pentatonic scale can be modified and moved anywhere on the fretboard, depending on the chord being played.*

The real magic of the pentatonic scale lies in its adaptability. The shape of the pentatonic scale in A minor can be moved anywhere on the fretboard to correspond to the chord that is being played.

For example, if you take that shape from the above chart and move it down to the third fret, it is now in the key of G minor. If you move it all the way down to the 12th fret, you're now playing the E minor pentatonic scale. The shape of the scale does not change at any fret position on the fretboard.

A Major Pentatonic

The minor pentatonic scale only works, however, over minor chords and power chords (we'll learn about those very soon). So, what happens when there is a major chord?

Tip 93: To modify the pentatonic scale for major chords, the root note is moved to the 4th finger on the sixth string of the pentatonic shape. Everything else stays the same.

So, if we wanted to modify the A minor pentatonic scale to the A major pentatonic scale, the fourth finger on the sixth string will now be on the fifth fret. The first finger is now on the second fret.

Here is the scale chart for the A major pentatonic:

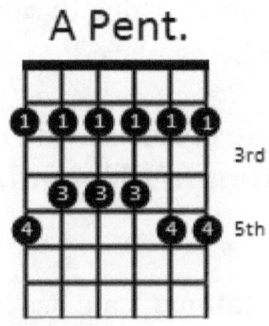

The 3rd and 5th frets are notated because that's where most guitars have fret markers, either small dots or square blocks, on the fretboard.

You can play any of these notes wherever an A major chord is being played. If you want to be a crazy electric guitar soloist, you'll want to get really good at playing the pentatonic shape. Practice it over and over again. Start slow, get smooth, and speed it up over time.

Also, keep in mind that the fourth string open is also an "A" note, the same as the fifth fret on the sixth string. Therefore, you can also utilize the open fourth string when experimenting with the A major pentatonic scale.

C Major Diatonic

Uh-oh. More big words. Fear not! Just like the pentatonic scale, the diatonic scale is a versatile scale pattern or shape that can be moved up and down the fretboard to fit any major key.

We'll get straight into the scale chart:

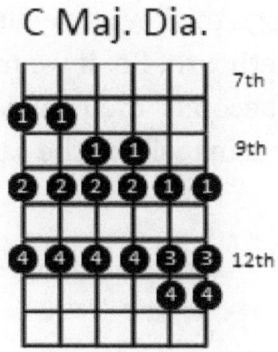

Once again, the 7th, 9th, and 12th frets are notated because those frets will most likely have fret markers on them.

To understand this shape, we'll break it down into three separate parts. The first part is on the sixth and fifth strings. Fingers one, two, and four play frets 8, 10, and 12, respectively.

Next, you move your first finger to the 9th fret on the fourth and third strings. The second finger still plays the 10th fret, and the fourth finger still plays the 12th fret.

Finally, move the first finger to the 10th fret for the second and first strings. The third finger now plays the 12th fret, and the fourth finger plays the 13th fret.

Tip 94: *Similar to the pentatonic, the diatonic shape can be moved anywhere on the fretboard to fit the corresponding key.*

The key of "C" is significant in this example because all of the notes played are, once again, whole notes. The first finger on the sixth string is playing a "C" note, which is the root note. The second finger on the same string is playing a "D" note, and the fourth finger on that string is playing an "E" note.

Once again, we can change the key as needed by moving this whole shape up or down the fretboard. So, if we move the whole shape up to that 10th fret, it now becomes the D major diatonic scale. The finger movement and spacing will be the same; only the frets change. Like this:

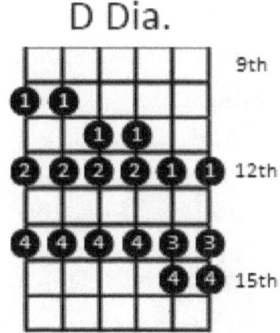

Notice that the finger placement hasn't changed, only where you start the pattern from. The 10th fret on the sixth string is a "D" note, which makes the whole scale in that key. If someone is playing a D major chord, you can play any note on this scale.

Using Scales

Tip 95: Memorize these shapes and patterns. Learn where they overlap and apply them alongside chord progressions.

It is not enough to simply learn; you must also apply what you have learned. The real trick to using scales is identifying where they overlap and using those overlapping notes to transition between scales during a chord progression.

For example, let's say we have an I-IV-V chord progression in the key of G major. That means we'll be starting with a G major chord, going to a C chord, then into a D chord, before repeating back to the G.

We can start by using our major pentatonic shape in the key of G. The fourth finger will start on that root "G" note on the third fret. Our first finger is now not utilized. Instead, it is the open notes. The G major pentatonic looks like this:

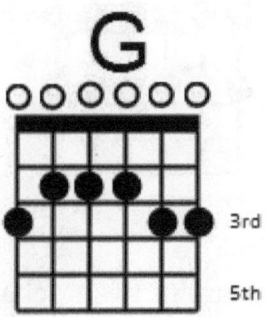

The fingers here aren't marked. You could use your first or second or whichever combination feels right to you as long as the G major chord is playing. You can play any of these notes to stay in that key.

But then, things change. The C chord is coming up. So, where do we go from here? Let's go back and look at our C major scale:

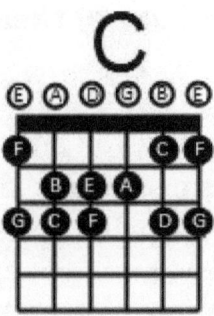

Notice a few notes that overlap? You can play these notes to transition from the G into the scale of C major. From here, you could also play notes in the C major diatonic scale:

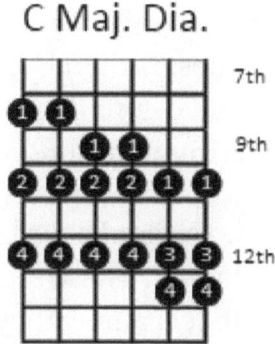

So now you're up here at the higher frets, and you know that a D chord is coming up next. What do you do? Shift everything up two frets and play around in the D major diatonic scale:

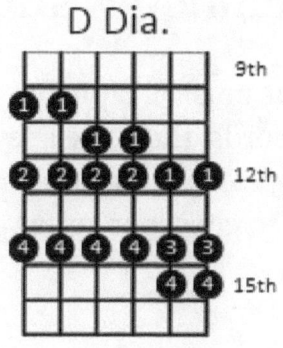

Of course, if you really have things down, you could also find the D major pentatonic scale on your own. Play around in there, and you should be able to find your way back down to the scale of G.

Tip 96: The most important thing about scales is to have fun with them.

Play notes up and down and in any random order. Find another guitarist to jam. Have them play simple chord progressions for you to practice transitioning scales. If there's no one around, try looking up backing tracks online. You can find any combination of keys and chord progressions to experiment around with.

Just like our lesson with chords and chord progressions, this is by no means a be-all-end-all lesson. These scales are merely a jumping-off point for you to learn how they work. Once you understand the concept, feel free to explore it on your own—research more scales. Play around with different shapes and melodies to your heart's content. But, again, these are merely your first steps into a larger world.

A Few More Techniques and Tricks

If notes are letters in our musical alphabet and scales are how to turn those letters into words, there are a few ways to add accents to how your instrument "speaks." Here are a few tips, tricks, and techniques you can use to give your guitar playing some flavor.

Slides

Simply put, slide your finger from one note to the next. For example, instead of using your third finger to transition to a new scale or pattern, just slide your first finger to that first note. Make sure you maintain pressure while sliding; otherwise, the note will die out. You can slide up, or you can slide down.

Bending and Vibrato

By bending the string either up or down while holding down the fret, you will change the pitch of the note. If you bend it hard enough, you will actually change the note to the next note higher. This will take some practice to get accurate, but it's a nifty trick to hit other notes on a scale.

Vibrato is quickly bending the string up and down to produce a "wavy" sound. The bend for a vibrato doesn't have to be extreme. In fact, the bend can be very subtle. Vibrato is great for the ends of phrases or melodies, like a punctuation mark at the end of a sentence.

Hammer-Ons

A hammer-on is accomplished by holding a note with one finger and quickly fingering another note on the same string on a higher fret. The impact of "hammering" the finger on the fretboard makes the note play without having to actually pick the string.

Hammer-on from the third fret to the fifth fret.

Here's another way of looking at it. First, play a note on the third fret of the sixth string using your first finger. Then quickly press down on the fifth fret with your third finger *without* strumming or picking the string. You should hear the note change if done correctly as your third finger presses down on the fret.

Hammer-ons can be accomplished with any consecutive note with any consecutive finger. So, for example, the second finger can hammer on after the first finger, the third after the second, and so on.

Experiment with hammer-ons when practicing your scales. Mastering this technique will allow you to really add texture and "feel" to your playing. It's essential if you want to play wicked fast solos.

Pull-Offs

Consider pull-offs like a reverse hammer on. The higher finger playing the higher note pulls off to the lower finger holding the lower note on the fretboard.

Pull-off from the fifth fret to the third fret.

If we look at the earlier example, and the third finger is on the fifth fret of the sixth string, the third finger pulls off that string while the first finger is still resting on the third fret.

Two key things to remember about pull-offs: First, the lower note must be held down before pulling off the higher note. Second, a slight upward or downward motion with the pulled-off finger helps the note play cleanly.

For the lower note to ring out, it has to be held down before the higher note is pulled off. Try to hold both notes at the same time before pulling off. Again, if we think of the third finger on the fifth fret, the first finger should already be pressing down on the third fret before the third finger pulls off.

Also, pulling off the fretboard in a straight upward motion might not let the lower note ring out clearly. If you move the higher finger in a slight up or down motion along the fretboard, the effect is similar to strumming the string with a pick. Think about "sweeping" the fretboard with the higher finger instead of just letting go of the note.

Picking Techniques

As you begin to master and speed up playing your scales, simple down stroking of the guitar pick just won't be enough. You will have to try out other styles of picking to accommodate.

Alternate picking is simply going both up and down with the guitar pick on a single string. You alternate between downstrokes and upstrokes. Remember to start slow and work on building speed over time. Use a metronome and try to hit your up-and-down strokes in time.

Tremolo picking is essentially alternate picking on overdrive. Single notes are played with rapid-fire up- and downstrokes. When tremolo picking is done fast enough and properly, the quick, repeated notes begin to sound like just one, constant sound. Think of surf rock, Latin guitar solos, and thrash metal to get an idea of tremolo picking.

Sweep picking is more akin to stringed instruments played with a bow, like a violin or a cello. In sweep picking, the guitar pick is moved across multiple strings as notes are played in rapid succession. In essence, the strumming hand moves more like strumming a chord, while the fretting fingers are quickly moving from note to note. For example, arpeggios in heavy metal guitar solos are often played with sweep picking.

To combine chords and single notes, you can use cross-picking. The low notes are played individually, while the higher notes on the thinner strings are strummed up and down. Cross picking creates a unique "bounce" in the rhythm. You'll find cross-picking all over rhythm guitars in country and bluegrass music.

Summary

- Scales are arrangements of notes in a certain order that allow you to create melodies.
- It's perhaps easiest to remember scales as a "road map" of notes, allowing you to go from one place to another on the fretboard.
- Scales can be shifted up or down on the fretboard to play higher or lower notes.
- Memorizing scales is the best way to learn where notes overlap with other scales to transition to different keys smoothly.
- Slides and bends, vibrato, hammer-ons, and pull-offs are just some of the ways to make your playing sound unique and add "flavor" to your melodies.

Chapter 8: Power Chords

Guitar solos never really resonated with me. I can definitely enjoy and appreciate the virtuosity that comes with a face-meltingly awesome solo; it was just never my style.

The guitarists that played solos, in my mind, were flashy, over-the-top, and borderline egotistical. Playing crazy-fast notes way high up on the neck just sounded like, "Hey! Look at what I can do!" in a braggadocious kind of way.

And I don't mean to demean or belittle if that's what you're into. Chase what ignites your soul and ignore the naysayers.

I always like to say that I graduated from the Punk Rock Academy of Power Chords. I loved heavy, distorted guitars that chugged along in syncopated rhythm. I wanted buzzsaw guitars locked in precision with insanely fast bass and drums. The more triplets, the better.

Power chords and rhythm are still my specialties, as I like to think. I might not be the fastest or most technical player, but I love what I play. And I play it with all my heart and soul.

Power chords, plain and simple, are the heart of rock and roll. Power chords are everywhere, from the earliest rock pioneers to the latest thrash metal. They're easy to learn, fun to play, and a must-have in every guitarist's arsenal.

Tip 97: Power chords are two or three-note chords consisting of a root note, a fifth note, and occasionally an octave note.

Think back to our lesson on scales, and let's begin with an E power chord. We'll use the open sixth string as our root "E" note. Count five notes from E, with E being "1." F is "2," G is "3," and so on. What note is the fifth?

If you answered "B," you are correct! So, we use the open "E" on the sixth string and the second fret on the fifth string as our "B" note. Then, the E power chord, using only the root and the fifth, looks like this:

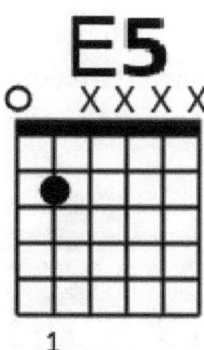

Here, a few things to notice: First, power chords are always named after the root note and the number "5," indicating the fifth note that is played. Second, we are only using our first finger to play the second fret of the fifth string. Thirdly, we are only playing the sixth and fifth strings. The rest of the strings are muted.

Tip 98: *A key technique to learn when playing power chords is to mute the strings you are not playing with your fretting hand fingers.*

You will lightly lay your first finger across the fourth through the first strings to mute the strings. Remember to play the note with the tip of your finger. Instead of trying to have your first finger curved, try to lay it flat across the fretboard. The first finger should lightly lay across the strings that are not played.

Practice getting those strings muted. Strum all six strings while playing only the open sixth string and the second fret of the fifth string. If you hear more than just those two notes, strum only the fourth through the first strings and figure out which strings need to be muted. You may also find that your first finger is pressing down *too hard*, and you're playing notes that you don't need to. Practice and find that balance.

Now, we will add in the additional octave chord. This is the same note as the root note, only played an octave higher. Can you go back to your scales and find it? Here is the three-note E power chord:

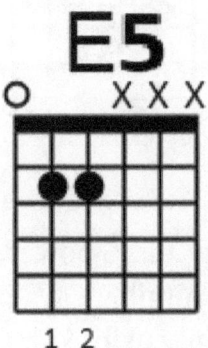

Did you get it right? Here again, we see that only three notes are being played, and the other three strings are muted. It's similar to the E major chord, just with the higher three strings muted.

E5 power chord. Only the sixth, fifth, and fourth strings are played.

Tip 99: Power chords are neither major nor minor in tonality.

Because power chords are simply a root note and a fifth note, there's no other note to give it the "happy" tone of a major chord or the "sad" tone of a minor. They can be considered neutral chords. This gives power chords incredible versatility. They can be played over the entire fretboard without having to worry about major or minor shifts.

We are now going to move over to the A power chord. The shape of the chord remains the same. We simply move the first and second fingers over one string. It looks like this:

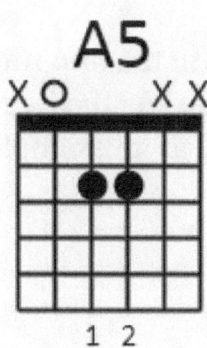

Again, notice the muted strings. For this chord, you can bring your thumb up and over to lightly lay it on the sixth string. Practice the transition between the E power chord and the A power chord. Take it slow, use different strumming patterns, and try to get the strings that aren't played muted as best as you can.

A5 power chord. The thumb blocks the sixth string, and only the fifth, fourth, and third strings are played.

Power Chords Down the Neck

You might be thinking to yourself, "Well, that's just the open strings. What about the rest of the neck?"

Tip 100: There is a specific hand shape when playing power chords down the neck. Learn the shape, and you've learned them all.

Power chords are played with the first finger on the root note, the third finger on the fifth note, and the fourth finger on the octave. Let's use the G power chord as an example:

G5

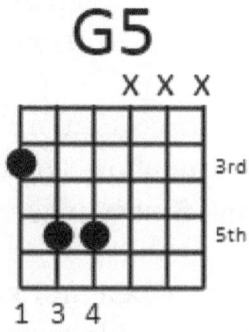

As you can see, the first finger is on the third fret of the sixth string, which is our root "G" note. The third finger is one string over and two frets down, the fifth fret of the fifth string. Finally, the fourth finger is simply the next string over on the same fret.

G5 power chord

You can move this shape *anywhere* along the neck of the guitar, and it will always be a power chord. First finger on the root, third finger one string over and two frets down, the fourth finger same fret one string over.

Want to play a B5? Put your first finger on the seventh fret and find the shape. How about a D5? Put your first finger on the tenth fret and find the shape. Sharp and flat notes can also be played as power chords.

Tip 101: Same as the E5 to A5 transition, power chords can also be played with the root note on the fifth string.

It is still vital to mute the strings that are not being played. For example, when playing power chords on the fifth string, you must mute the sixth, second, and first strings.

You have a couple of options when muting the sixth string. Same as the open A5 chord, you may be able to use your thumb to mute the sixth string. However, this may cause rounding of the entire hand for some guitarists, making it difficult to mute the second and first strings.

You can also use the very tip of your first finger to just barely touch the sixth string. As long as enough of your finger blocks the vibration of the string, it will be muted. Again, this may prove difficult to some guitarists. You might not be able to maintain adequate pressure on the first finger to play the right note while, at the same time, muting the sixth string.

Another option to mute the sixth string is to use the second finger. If your fingers are long enough, you may find that the second finger naturally extends far enough to reach the sixth string. If this is the case, you can use that reach to lightly lay the second finger on the sixth string and mute it.

C5 power chord. Left: the second finger blocks the sixth string. Right: thumb blocks the sixth string. Use whatever is most comfortable for you.

Tip 102: When moving to different power chords, relax the hand but maintain the shape.

The easiest way to transition power chords up and down the neck is to relax the fretting hand but keep the fingers in the same power chord shape. It's far more difficult to completely let go of the neck, move your hand, and try to reshape your fingers into the right position.

Keep in mind that the spacing between frets gets smaller as you move down the neck. Therefore, you will have to adjust the spacing between your fingers to accommodate this change. Just try to drill in your mind (and your hand): the first finger on the root note, third finger one string over two frets down, fourth finger one string over the same fret.

Palm Muting

There is another technique that, in certain genres, goes hand-in-hand with power chords. It's called palm muting.

Tip 103: Palm-muting is placing the side of your strumming hand on the strings near the bridge to slightly mute the strings.

When performed correctly, the chords will sound slightly muffled and quieter. In addition, you'll often find palm muting done during verses or "softer" parts of songs. This gives those songs a dynamic range without the use of effects.

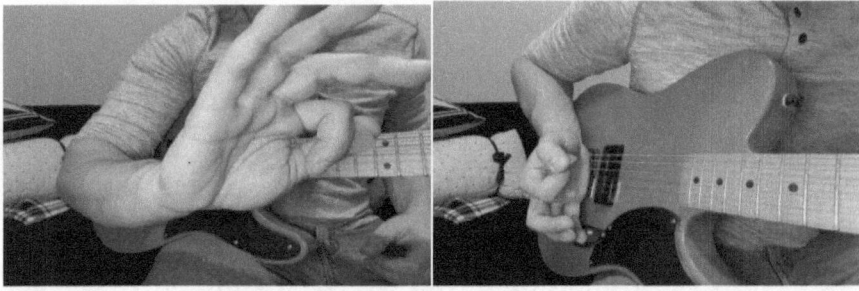

Palm muting. Left: the side of the strumming hand is used in palm muting.
Right: proper palm muting placement. Don't use the entire palm.

To palm mute, lightly place the side of your strumming hand slightly above where the strings leave the bridge. It's not your entire palm, just the side of it. Turn your hand down towards the body of the guitar and strum with your pick.

At first, learning to palm mute properly can be quite tricky. There is a certain "sweet spot" that has to be found. Press down too hard with the strumming hand; the notes will be too muted and will sound cut off. Press too lightly, and the effect will be barely noticeable.

In addition, the "sweet spot" will vary from guitar to guitar. The scale length, bridge type, and body construction will change where the palm mute sounds best. You may have to move your hand closer to or farther away from the bridge. Once you have the fundamentals down, like any other skill, the transition to a different guitar will be much easier.

Tip 104: Experiment with different strumming patterns after finding the sweet spot and getting comfortable with palm muting.

It is possible to both upstroke and downstroke while palm muting. It might help to think about "sweeping" the pick across the strings while keeping your strumming hand muting the bridge. You can also focus on hitting just the strings you are trying to play to make the movement smaller and more controlled.

Another fun thing to do with palm muting is adding accent notes in your strumming pattern. You can alternate between having the chords be muted or unmuted while you're strumming.

Remember back to our strumming and rhythm count of "1-and-2-and-3-and-4." Palm mute and use all downstrokes to play on every count. On the "2" and on the "4," lift your palm up slightly to let the chord play completely open before putting your palm back down. Take a look at this table for reference:

Count:	1	and	2	and	3	and	4	and
	X	X	O	X	X	X	O	X

On the "X's," play the power chord palm muted. On the "O's," play the power chord fully without the palm mute. Start slowly and gradually increase speed. Feel how the strings rest under your strumming hand. Move your hand to see how the palm-muted sound changes—experiment with when to palm mute and when to play the chord fully.

Tip 105: *The goal with palm muting is to be as comfortable and relaxed as possible.*

At first, this will seem nearly impossible. You may find yourself tensing up your strumming hand or pressing down on the strings too hard. The palm mute might sound clicky because your hand is too far up and away from the bridge. The palm mute might not register at all because you're not putting enough of your palm on the strings.

As with all things, it just takes time and practice. Listen to songs that utilize palm muting for inspiration. Learn how to groove and stay "in the pocket" of the rhythm. Don't stress about it or beat yourself up if you don't get it right away. Practice, experiment, and have fun with palm muting.

Power Chord Progressions and Patterns

Similar to scales and chord progressions, certain patterns and orders of power chords sound best played together. We could formally look at these patterns, like the Roman numerals we looked at earlier. But there's another way of looking at the shapes of these power chord progressions along the neck.

The "L" Progression

Tip 106: The first power chord progression consists of three power chords, played one after another, in an "L" shape on the neck.

For example, we can begin on the third fret of the sixth string with a G power chord. Strum that power chord four times. Then, move one string over, with the first finger on the third fret of the sixth string, and play the C power chord four times. Finally, move up two frets on the same string to the fifth fret. That's a D power chord. Play it four times.

G5 to C5 to D5 progression. The dot marks the first finger's position of the power chord. Notice how it sort of moves in an "L" shape?

Notice how the power chords move in an "L" shape on the fretboard? There are a few cool things you can do here. First, you can play any of these chords in any combination. They all fit in the same key, so they will all sound good together. Secondly, you can move this shape anywhere along the neck. Try it! Start on the sixth fret of the sixth string, move to the sixth fret of the fifth string, and then on to the eighth fret of the fifth string.

Get a feel for this progression—play along with a metronome. Change up strumming patterns. Add in palm muting. Chances are, if you have a good ear, you might hear a song or two you recognize that also use this pattern.

The Extended "L" Progression

Tip 107: The "L" progression can be extended for one more power chord, up two more frets after the third chord, for a total of four power chords.

We can go back to our first example, the G to C to D power chord progression. After you play the D power chord on the fifth fret, move up two more frets. Play the E power chord, rooted on the seventh fret of the fifth string, four times. After that, you can go back down to the G.

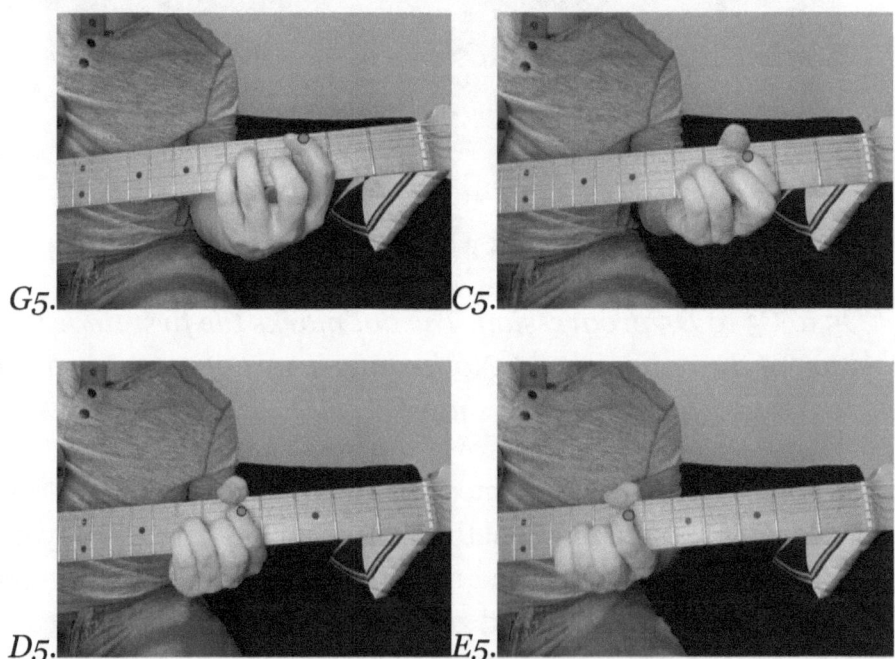

G5 to C5 to D5 to E5 progression. Again, follow the dot.

This is another common progression used in a lot of pop and rock songs. Same as the first progression, you can play these chords in any combination or at any position along the neck.

The "X" Progression

Tip 108: The "X" progression, similar to the extended "L" progression, contains four chords, except this time we move in an "X"-like pattern on the neck.

We can once again start with the G power chord on the third fret of the sixth string. Strum four times. Now, play the D power chord on the fifth fret of the fifth string. After that, move back to the sixth string on the same fifth fret. That's an A power chord. Finally, go to the third fret, only this time you'll be on the fifth string. Strum that C power chord four times, and you can go back to the beginning.

G5.   C5.

G5 to C5 to A5 to E5 "X" progression

Again, if you visualize the movement of the power chord on the fretboard, you should be able to tell that it moves in kind of an "X" shape. Just like the two "L" progressions, any combination of chords can be used in any order. You can also move the shape anywhere on the neck and start it from any position.

The "T" Progression

Tip 109: The "T" progression is another four-chord progression, starting with one power chord on the sixth string and three chords on the fifth string.

For the "T" progression, we are actually going to start on the fifth fret of the sixth string with an A power chord. The second chord is the D power chord, one string over on the fifth fret of the fifth string. Next, move up two frets to the seventh fret on the fifth string and play the E power chord. Finally, go all the way down to the third fret on the same fifth string and play the C power chord.

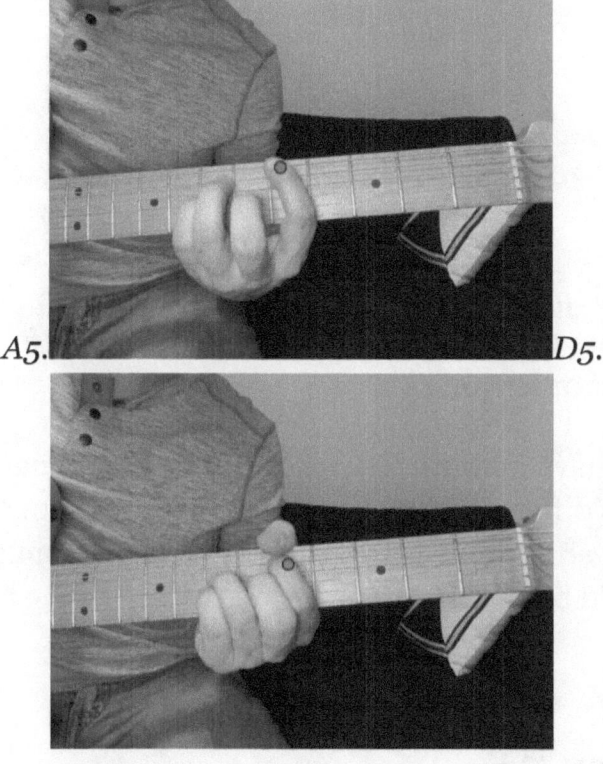

A5.   D5.

The pattern should be fairly obvious at this point. The power chords move around the neck in a shape similar to the letter "T." Just like the three other progressions, you can start it on any fret or use the chords in any order you like.

Remember: have fun with the progressions. Experiment around with them in different areas of the neck. Practice with a metronome. Try different strumming patterns, along with palm muting. Power chords should be a blast!

Summary

- If the city was built on rock and roll, then rock and roll was built on power chords.

- Power chords consist of three notes: a root note, a fifth, and an octave.
- Power chords can be played anywhere along the neck of the guitar on the sixth or fifth strings.
- Palm-muting is using the side of the palm of your strumming hand to slightly mute the strings.
- Power chord progressions can be looked at as different shapes or patterns on the neck of the guitar, such as L, X, or T.

Chapter 9: Reading Guitar Tab

After asking if I was interested in being in his band, Chuck invited me over to his house for a little jam session. Just try to gloss over the fact that a grown man was inviting a 17-year-old kid to his house to play guitar. I have no idea why my parents didn't throw a bigger fuss. I probably lied to them.

Chuck and I sat on his back porch in the humid Florida evening air. We conversed about bands we both loved. He grew up listening to punk rock bands that originated in Southern California in the early and mid-'90s. I loved the bands that were inspired by those bands, pop-punk and emo bands from the late '90s and early '00s.

So, every song we played that night, we both knew because they all essentially came from the same pedigree. I luckily had done my fair share of self-study at this point. The internet provided plenty of guitar tablature to learn from. I knew what songs I liked, which ones I wanted to play, and I learned them. Those songs just so happened to be ones that Chuck also knew.

Thanks to my musical background in chorus class, I was also able to sing in harmony with Chuck's vocal melody. He was impressed, he told me. Not many people could sing backup vocals like that. I just enjoyed the sound of a well-placed two-part vocal harmony, and I was happy to provide.

Then, he decided to show me some of his original songs. He said if I couldn't pick it up the first couple go-arounds, that was okay. But, of course, he wasn't expecting much from a 17-year-old kid.

I learned three songs on the spot and came up with brand new backup harmonies. Chuck and I have been brothers bonded in music ever since.

Guitar tablature (or tab) is one of the most common forms of guitar notation. It is the most effective way to write down and read music for guitar in most cases. It is also the most widely available. Several websites offer free guitar tabs to view and download; there are also several mobile apps and computer programs for writing and downloading guitar tabs. Professional guitar tab books can also be purchased if you prefer a more traditional format.

Tip 110: In guitar tablature, there are six horizontal lines. These represent the six strings of your guitar. The bottom line is the guitar's sixth (thickest) string, and the top line is the first (thinnest) string. So guitar tab will look something like this:

```
e | -----------------
B | -----------------
G | -----------------
D | -----------------
A | -----------------
E | -----------------
```

A helpful way to remember this is to lay your guitar face-up on your lap. If you look at the strings along the neck, the sixth string is on the bottom. Guitar tab is like a frontal view of the strings on the neck.

On the lines, there will be numbers. Those numbers represent the frets on the guitar. A "1" would be the first fret, "2" is the second, and so on. Unlike chord charts or certain scale charts, guitar tab does not tell you which finger to use on which fret.

For example, if you see a "3" on the top line of the guitar tab, that means you would play the third fret on the first string. You could use any finger you want. It may depend on what notes come before or after that particular note. For example, you may use your first finger if the next note is on the fifth fret, or you may use your third finger if the note before was the first fret. This is why it's important to practice your scales and get used to moving your fingers around the fretboard.

You may also see a number zero ("0") on the lines. As you might be able to guess, that means you would play that string open, with no fingers on that string. So, for example, if there is a "0" on the bottom line, you play the sixth (thickest) string open.

Tip 111: When you see numbers written above or below each other in the same vertical space, those notes are played together in a chord.

This can be any combination of numbers, more than two but no more than six. The easiest way to understand this is by demonstrating a chord we are already familiar with. Let's look at the G major chord chart:

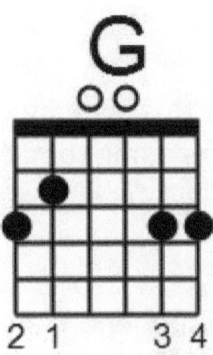

This chord should be plenty familiar displayed in this manner. But how does it look in guitar tablature form? Like this:

```
e | - 3 - - - - - - - - - - - - -
B | - 3 - - - - - - - - - - - - -
G | - 0 - - - - - - - - - - - - -
D | - 0 - - - - - - - - - - - - -
A | - 2 - - - - - - - - - - - - -
E | - 3 - - - - - - - - - - - - -
```

Each horizontal line is a string, and each number is a fret. If all of the numbers are directly above or below each other, that is one chord with all of the notes played together.

Tip 112: On guitar tablature, you will often see individual notes alongside these chords.

We can continue to look at the G major chord. Only this time, we will play each note of the chord individually before playing the chord itself. Take a look at this tab, and play along:

```
e | - - - - - - - - - - - 3 - 3 - -
B | - - - - - - - - - 3 - - - 3 - -
G | - - - - - - 0 - - - - - 0 - -
D | - - - - 0 - - - - - - - 0 - -
A | - - 2 - - - - - - - - - 2 - -
E | 3 - - - - - - - - - - - 3 - -
```

Remember that a guitar tab tells you which frets to play, not which fingers to play them with. In the above example, your fretting hand fingers will make the G major chord shape and hold it. The strumming hand plays the individual notes, starting at the sixth string, playing each individual note in succession. Once you play the final note on the highest string, you'll strum the chord in its entirety. Just understand that notes stacked together on the same vertical line are all played together as a chord.

Tip 113: One of the downsides to guitar tablature is that it does not show the timing or the rhythm of the notes.

For the above example, with the individual notes of the G chord, you have no way of knowing how fast to play it or how long to hold each individual note before playing the next one. So, when you start looking at tabs for songs you want to play, you will have to listen to the song while you look at the tab.

It is important that you listen to a song while you are learning it, obviously. You should be paying attention to how the notes in the song sound compared to the notes you are playing. If you want to learn a song by reading the tab, listen to that song a lot. You want to be able to notice your own mistakes when you start playing along.

Tip 114: You don't need to know how to read sheet music to play guitar.

Traditional music notation or sheet music will be written above the tab on some professionally prepared or published guitar tabs. If you can already read sheet music, then that's great! It will definitely help you with the timing of the notes.

If you can't read sheet music, that is totally fine. You will just have to really listen to the song you are learning and pay attention to your own playing. You must figure out the rhythm and the timing of the notes on your own. On the plus side, you'll likely become really good at learning things by ear once you've developed that skill.

Tip 115: There are some pros and cons when using guitar tablature over traditional sheet music.

A benefit to guitar tablature is that it shows you exactly where on the neck to play a note. Traditional sheet music only shows what note to play.

Let's say that the sheet music instructs you to play a high "E" note. Obviously, that can be played with the open first string. However, it can also be played on the fifth fret of the second string, the ninth fret of the third string, the fourteenth fret of the fourth string, or the nineteenth fret of the fifth string. Try it! It's the same note! Sheet music doesn't tell you which fret to play. Guitar tablature does.

Conversely, on the downside, most online guitar tabs lack definitive standards or guidelines for their notations. Different sites may have tabs that look slightly different or indicate certain techniques in different ways. We'll cover some common notations here.

First, in the tab examples that we've shown so far, the letters to the left of the guitar tab indicate the tuning of each string. So, from top to bottom, we have "e, B, G, D, A, E in standard tuning."

```
e | - - - - - - - - - - - - - - - -
B | - - - - - - - - - - - - - - - -
G | - - - - - - - - - - - - - - - -
D | - - - - - - - - - - - - - - - -
A | - - - - - - - - - - - - - - - -
E | - - - - - - - - - - - - - - - -
```

However, some guitar tabs will indicate alternate tunings. For example, if you are looking at a guitar tab for a song that is in drop D tuning, the tab might look like this:

```
e | - - - - - - - - - - - - - - - -
B | - - - - - - - - - - - - - - - -
G | - - - - - - - - - - - - - - - -
D | - - - - - - - - - - - - - - - -
A | - - - - - - - - - - - - - - - -
D | - - - - - - - - - - - - - - - -
```

Notice how the bottom line has a "D" as opposed to standard tuning's "E." That is because, in drop D tuning, the sixth string is tuned a full step down to a "D."

This isn't always the case. Sometimes, guitar tabs will have the specific tuning listed in the tab description or at the very beginning of the tab document. So, if you see just the lines of the tab with no letters to the left, check the description of the tab to see what tuning the song is in. For example, it might read "Standard," "Drop D," "Half Step Down," or some other tuning.

Tip 116: Remember our tricks and techniques from Chapter 7? Guitar tab will also show you when to use those techniques.

We can start with hammer-ons. Hammer-ons can be indicated by the letters "h.o." or more commonly by just the letter "h." Take a look at this tab:

```
e | ----------------
B | ----------------
G | -3 h 5 ----------
D | ----------------
A | ----------------
E | ----------------
```

In this example, you would play the third fret of the third string and then hammer on the fifth fret of the same string. Which fingers you use are up to you, but you would most likely use the first and third fingers.

The opposite of a hammer-on, the pull-off, is indicated by either the letters "p.o." or just the letter "p." Here is an example of how a pull-off would look in tab form:

```
e | ----------------
B | ----------------
G | -5 p 3 ----------
D | ----------------
A | ----------------
E | ----------------
```

Here we have the opposite of the hammer-on example. Play the fifth fret of the third string, and then pull off to the third fret of the same string. Again, which fingers you use are at your discretion. Maybe you could try it with your fourth and second fingers this time?

Bends are a little more difficult. A bend is appropriately indicated by the letter "b." Bends might also be indicated by the "^" symbol. You will have a fret number, the letter "b" or the symbol "^," and then another fret number after it. Like so:

```
e | ----------------
B | ----------------
G | --7 b 9 ----------
D | ----------------
A | ----------------
E | ----------------
```

You will start by playing the seventh fret of the third string. Then, you will bend the string either up or down until it reaches the same pitch as if you were playing the ninth fret. It may help to first play the note at the ninth fret, listen to the sound, and go back down to the seventh fret. On a guitar tab, it will look like this:

```
e | - - - - - - - - - - - - - - - -
B | - - - - - - - - - - - - - - - -
G | - - 7 b 9 r 7 - - - - - - - - -
D | - - - - - - - - - - - - - - - -
A | - - - - - - - - - - - - - - - -
E | - - - - - - - - - - - - - - - -
```

To play this, you play the note on the seventh fret of the third string. Then, bend the note up or down until it reaches the same pitch as the note on the ninth string. Finally, unbend the note back down to the original note on the seventh fret.

Tip 117: Vibrato can also be shown on guitar tab.

It is notated as either the letter "v" or by the "~" symbol. See this example:

```
e | - - - - - - - - - - - - - - - -
B | - - - - - - - - - - - - - - - -
G | - - 7 v - - - - - - - - - - - -
D | - - - - - - - - - - - - - - - -
A | - - - - - - - - - - - - - - - -
E | - - - - - - - - - - - - - - - -
```

Here again, we start on the seventh fret. The "v" tells us to vibrato that note by bending it slightly up and down. How quickly you do it depends on the song. Some vibrato bends are fast and shallow. Others are long and slow, similar to bends. As we discussed before, tablature lacks the rhythm and timing notations of traditional sheet music. So again, listening to the song you are learning by reading tab is key.

Slides are written on a guitar tab using slash symbols. The direction of the slide is notated by which slash symbol is used. A forward-slash ("/") is a slide up, and a backward slash ("\") is a slide down.

If the slide ends at a particular fret, that will also be noted. See if you can understand this tab:

```
e | - - - - - - - - - - - - - - - -
B | - - - - - - - - - - - - - - - -
G | - - 5 / 7 - - 7 \ 5 - - - - -
D | - - - - - - - - - - - - - - - -
A | - - - - - - - - - - - - - - - -
E | - - - - - - - - - - - - - - - -
```

Do you think you got it? Here's what the tab is telling you. First, play the fifth fret on the third string. Then, slide your finger up to the seventh fret. Next, play the note at the seventh fret, and then slide back down to the fifth fret.

Tip 118: Palm-muting has its own notation on guitar tablature.

Appropriately, palm muting is notated on the guitar tab with "p.m." either above or below the notes being played. There will be dashes that will show you how long to palm mute for. Have a look at this guitar tab with palm muting:

```
e | - - - - - - - - - - - - - - - - -
B | - - - - - - - - - - - - - - - - -
G | - - - - - - - - - - - - - - - - -
D | - 2 - 2 - 2 - - - 2 - 2 - 2 - -
A | - 2 - 2 - 2 - - - 2 - 2 - 2 - -
E | - 0 - 0 - 0 - - - 0 - 0 - 0 - -
      p.m.---|      p.m.---|
```

In this tab, you are playing the E power chord six times. The first two are palm-muted, then you play the third open. That pattern then repeats, two E power chords palm-muted and one power chord open. Makes sense, right?

You think you've got it all now? Test out your tab-reading skills with this simple song and see if you can recognize the melody:

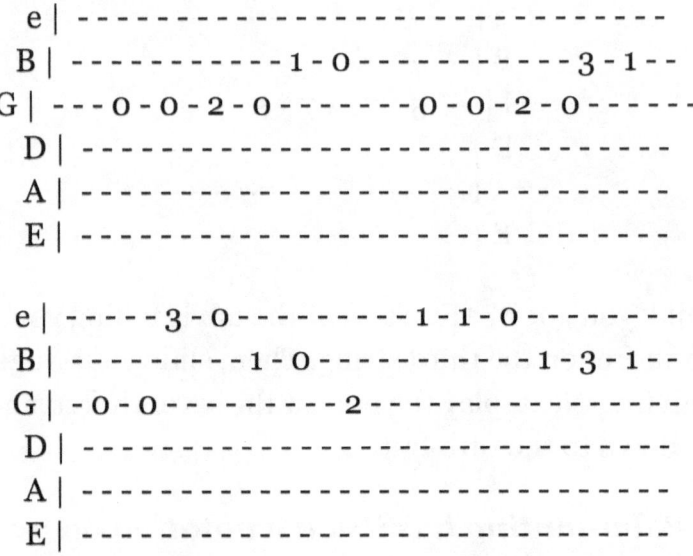

Did you get it? How did it sound? Were you able to get the right timing of the notes?

Tip 119: *No two tabs are written the same way.*

For example, someone else may have chosen to start the song on the fifth fret of the fourth string in the above song. It's the same musical note, so it's not technically wrong. However, it is imperative that you listen to the song you're playing to make sure you are playing it correctly.

If you are learning a song and are having particular difficulty with the tab you are learning from, try looking the tab up on a different website. Another author of another tab may have interpreted the song differently and written it in a different spot. Also, some guitar tabs for the same song might have different tunings. For example, one tab may have the first note on the third fret of the sixth string in standard tuning, while another has the first note as the fifth fret of the sixth string, except it's in drop D tuning. But, again, both are the same note (a "G" in this example); they are just in different tunings.

Summary

- Guitar tablature is a type of music notation that shows what frets to play on guitar. It requires no knowledge of how to read traditional sheet music.
- There are six horizontal lines on the guitar tablature, representing the individual strings of the guitar. Numbers on the lines will show which fret to play on which string. A number zero ("0") indicates an open string.
- Numbers that are grouped together in a straight vertical line are a chord; they are all strummed in one continuous motion.
- Certain techniques, such as bends, vibrato, hammer-ons, and pull-offs, have their own specific notations on guitar tablature.
- Be aware that there are some downsides to guitar tablature. It does not show rhythmic or timing information. Although it is widely available online, not all guitar tablature is accurate.

Chapter 10: Now What?

There was a time in my life when, sadly, I decided to step away from playing guitar in a band. I thought I had to push away "childish" things, like playing rock 'n' roll in a band. So instead, I focused on what I thought I needed to do to become a mature, responsible adult.

Let me be clear; I regret none of it. But, I never strayed too far away from playing guitar. I always had one or two lying around wherever I lived. It was always a fun party trick to whip out an acoustic and play along to whatever music was playing.

I became fortunate to become pretty financially secure. My mature, responsible adulting had paid off, so to speak. One day, while browsing online, I saw something I could not pass up,

a signature guitar that I had wanted since I had first started playing guitar. It was specifically designed to the exact specifications of the guitarist that had first inspired me to start playing guitar. I had to have it.

So, I bought it.

Once I finally had it in my possession, I was so happy. I meticulously unboxed it, enjoying the slow unwrapping of the padded packing paper. I played it as often as I could, along with all the artist's albums of that signature guitar.

I had kept in touch with Chuck over the years. I sent him a picture of the guitar. "That's awesome!" he told me. It was serendipitous that I should send him that picture.

He went on to tell me he was thinking about getting the old band back together.

I was very interested.

The information and tips contained in this book are merely the first steps into a much larger world. Hopefully, you've stayed consistent and practiced hard.

But, you may find yourself wondering where to go from here. Don't worry. Many guitarists have been in that same position. The jump from beginner to amateur is intimidating but completely worth it.

Tip 120: Research, explore, and study every guitar resource you can.

There are plenty of sources of information on how to play guitar.

Today is truly a golden age for guitarists. The internet provides so many wonderful resources to learn how to play guitar. Both free and paid resources are available to you.

Hopefully, this book has given you a head start on your guitar journey. But, again, it is by no means a be-all-end-all resource. If you want to learn more about scales, research scales. Find a website that offers lessons specifically for guitar scales. If you want to learn more about power chords, do a quick internet search for "power chord songs for beginners" and learn some of those.

A true expert never stops learning. Find more books to read. See if your favorite band has a biography or even a book written by the band themselves. Watch interviews of famous guitarists. Listen to the music that inspired them. Chinese poet Matsuo Bashō said, "Do not seek to follow in the footsteps of the wise. Seek what they sought."

Tip 121: Listen to music of every genre.

It's incredibly easy to stay in our own bubble. We find what we like, and we stick with it. There's nothing inherently wrong with that.

However, if you want to continue to grow as a guitarist, you will have to explore outside of your comfortable musical bubble. You don't even have to like what you find out there necessarily. But you should at least try to appreciate what is being done.

Listen to jazz, country, R&B, pop, hip-hop, and everything in between. You'd be surprised at how many heavy metal guitarists list classical composers like Beethoven and Bach as their inspirations.

Something incredible happens when you explore outside what you already know. You absorb it and interpret it based on your own experience and expectations on some subconscious level. Then, when it comes time to sit down and play your own instrument, the things you listen to will unknowingly come back to you in some surprising ways.

In addition, when you listen to other musical genres, you'll find more similarities than you might imagine. Chord progressions will often overlap among genres. The "I-V-vi-IV" progression is referred to as the most popular progression. Learn it, and then carefully listen to pop, rock, and even country songs. You will be amazed at how many songs use that chord progression.

Tip 122: Train and trust your ears.

It might seem trivial to have to say this, but since music is an auditory art form, you have to develop your auditory senses. Therefore, you should listen with intention to the music you listen to and yourself.

Recognize the different instruments played in a song. Appreciate the interplay between the drum and bass. Figure out what the guitar is doing in relation to the vocals. Identify any other instruments or sounds on the track. What emotion does the song evoke? How do the instruments relay that emotion?

This also goes back to listening to different genres. They all have their own specialized techniques and styles. Try to understand and appreciate those differences. When you think of a song like a tapestry or a collage, you can pick out the interwoven parts and see how they interrelate with one another.

Don't let your "good enough" be good enough when it comes to your own playing. Listen carefully to what you're playing and how it sounds. If you think it doesn't sound quite right, figure out why. Maybe it's something as simple as needing to tune your guitar. Maybe there's something with your technique that you need to improve. Be your own best critic.

Tip 123: Don't compare yourself to others.

Comparison is the thief of joy, or so it's said. So naturally, you will want to be just as good as your guitar heroes or even just as good as the best guitarists in your local area. However, you have to keep in mind that your journey is just beginning. Everyone has to start somewhere.

It's okay to want to play like another person. Maybe you admire their style, their sound, or some other aspect. Never forget that you are the only you that exists. Embrace your influences and find your own way.

When you first start, it will be normal to duplicate your idols. That's okay. It's part of the process of learning what you like. But don't be beholden to stay in that same style, genre, or way of playing. Instead, explore and discover other guitarists that you can chase after, so to speak.

No matter how far along you get or how good your technique becomes, there will always be someone out there that can do something "better" than you can. Even the greatest guitarists in the world will see something that impresses them and makes them say, "Wow, that is some great guitar playing!" One day, maybe you can be that inspiration to someone else!

But, for now, just enjoy the journey.

Tip 124: *Take your time and stay consistent.*

You're going to want to learn the next thing as quickly as you can, whatever that next thing may be. But be patient with yourself. You will stumble, and you will struggle. But, again, it's just part of the process. Give yourself a break from time to time, but always come back to it. If you really love playing guitar, the "come back to it" part will just come naturally.

In another sense, don't rush through learning the steps, either. The chapters in this book are laid out in order for a good reason. Take everything one step at a time. Don't move on to the next step until you have a firm footing on the step you're already on. Moving too fast is the easiest way to hit a performance plateau.

A "performance plateau" is when you can't seem to get any upward progression on whatever skill you are working on. If you find yourself hitting a plateau, your best bet is usually to take a step backward and work on something fundamental. Often, a plateau is caused because you lack enough proficiency in some skill or technique to progress. You might not think that the basics matter, but they absolutely do.

Take it slow when building the foundations of your guitar playing. A house is only as sturdy as the foundations it's built on. So, don't speed through any of the basics. Master those first before moving on.

Don't burn yourself out by playing for hours on the weekend, only to lose the motivation to play during the week. Small, consistent practice sessions are far better than only one- or two-hour jams. Think about it this way: if you practice only one hour on Saturday and another hour on Sunday, you're only practicing about 100 hours in a year. But, on the other hand, if you practice 30 minutes every single day, you nearly double the amount of time you practice in a single year!

If you stay consistent and practice every single day, you're more likely to build on the skills you are learning. For example, if you were to only play on the weekends, you'd spend more time trying to remember what you practiced the week before than actually learning something new.

Carve out that 30 minutes every single day and look forward to it. Take away any distractions you might have, and only focus on playing the guitar. Those 30 minutes will probably become the most enjoyable half-hour of your day. The more you enjoy it, the more likely you are to stick with it.

The key is to do just that: stick with it. The first three to six months might be boring, and you'll find yourself wanting to do more and go faster. However, it is far better to go slow and consistent than to go fast and loose.

Tip 125: Try other stringed instruments.

Recall back to Chapter 1 when we discussed that a guitar is classified as a chordophone. Once you feel you have a solid grasp of the fundamentals of playing guitar, you might be surprised to find how easy it is for you to learn and play other instruments.

Bass guitar

First, and likely the simplest instrument to transition to after learning guitar, is the bass guitar. The bass guitar has a longer neck and thicker strings to allow for a lower range of notes to be played. There are only four strings as opposed to the standard guitar's six. The parts of the bass are essentially the same (head, neck, and body) and basically all perform the same function. Learning how to play bass is also the most logical because nearly every band that has a guitar in it will also need a bass player.

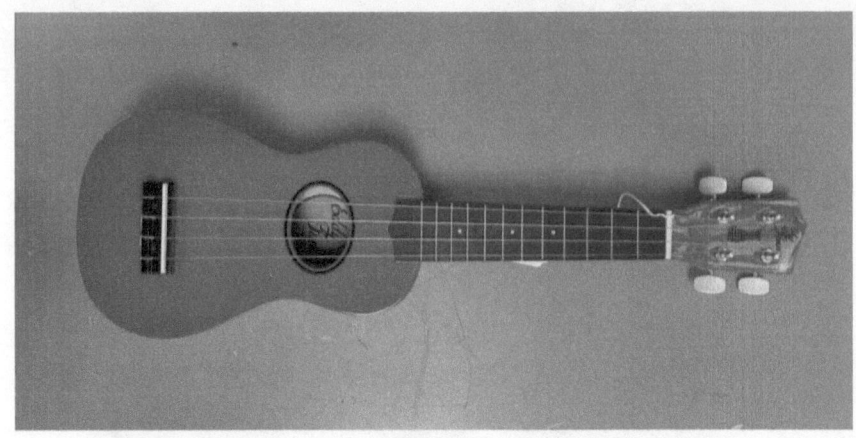
Ukulele

Another instrument that's fairly easy to transition to is the ukulele. A ukulele is basically a smaller, four-stringed acoustic guitar. The tuning of the strings is a bit different, so the chord shapes you've learned for guitar won't directly carry over to the ukulele. But it still offers the familiar fretted neck setup of your traditional guitar. It's a fun and quirky instrument to try.

Some other stringed instruments to try after guitar include the banjo, the lap or pedal steel guitar, and the mandolin. But don't stop at stringed instruments, either. Tap a few keys on a piano. Pick up a harmonica and give it a blow. If you find yourself air-drumming while you're learning a song, give the drums a shot.

Tip 126: There's no shame in getting one-on-one lessons.

You might find yourself in a difficult spot. Something doesn't "click" with whatever you're trying to learn. Or maybe you feel like you've gained all you can from reading this book or watching tutorials online.

Try a lesson or two with a local guitar tutor. Let them know you've been studying on your own and want to learn more. Showing your own initiative to seek out lessons instead of self-study will be a breath of fresh air to many a tutor!

You may have to swallow your pride a bit in order to walk into a guitar lesson to ask for help. But, if you really are struggling, it will totally be worth it. Even if you aren't struggling, getting a guitar lesson or two might still be beneficial. I know of a few guitarists that had played for years and were pretty good on their own; still, go and get guitar lessons to learn something new or refine a technique.

Besides, nothing compares to the immediate feedback of having someone sitting right across from you, giving you insight on a skill that they are intimately familiar with. Of course, you can learn almost anything from books and videos online. But, it still isn't the same as having a tutor or a coach there, in person, to guide you along the way.

Tip 127: HAVE FUN!

Your author onstage (2021)

Of all the tips in this book, this might be the most important one.

Playing guitar (or any instrument, really) should be driven by passion. Many skills are developed in tandem with learning how to play guitar, like hand-eye coordination. In addition, just listening to music improves mental well-being, and playing music helps even more.

In the end, playing guitar should be enjoyable. You might have to force yourself to practice every once in a while, but it should never become a chore. The guitar should be an outlet for your joy, sadness, pain, and triumph. You were drawn to it for a reason. Never lose hold of that.

Music is meant to be shared. Find others that share the same passion for music as you. That doesn't even necessarily mean starting a band. Seek out other guitarists that just want to hang out and jam. Play your guitar for your family and friends.

Learn to write your own music. Experiment with new chord shapes and progressions. Seek out new scales and modes to discover new melodies.

Remember that not everyone that plays guitar has to be a musician signed to a big record label deal. Instead, you can expand your knowledge and become a guitar technician. Maybe you're the entrepreneurial type, and you can open your own local guitar store. Or perhaps you can audition to be a session guitarist for stage musicals or small recording studios.

Above all else, follow your passion. Your heart, soul, guiding light, or whatever you want to call it will lead the way. Stay true to yourself and chase what gets your heart racing.

Keep on playing.

Epilogue

My life has been through many ups and downs. I've had friends come and go, and I've lived under many different roofs. However, the one thing that has always stayed constant in my life is music.

Music was my safe harbor when times got rough, and it was my celebration when times were worth celebrating. As a result, nearly every memory I have from my early days is colored with the music of the time.

Playing guitar has brought me so much joy over the years. Through this book, I hope you can also find some kind of joy by playing guitar.

While writing, I often thought to myself, "What would I go back and tell myself when I was first starting to play?" So I tried to write the book I would have wanted when I was learning how to play. At the beginning of my journey, I read through countless online articles and checked out a book or two from the library on how to play guitar. Through that method, I had devised my own path to guitar-playing prowess.

Each lesson or article I read only held pieces and fragments of information that eventually came together for me. It took me so long to figure it all out. So, again, I hope that your guitar-playing journey is made just a little less strenuous and a little more enjoyable by reading my book.

Every story I've told in this book is one hundred percent true. There are so many more happy memories that I have been fortunate to create, thanks to a guitar in my hands. I've made lifelong relationships because of the guitar that I am forever grateful for.

So, let's go back to 17-year-old Norm...

When I went back to Chuck's to meet the rest of the band, I was beyond nervous. Chuck had given me a demo CD of 4 or 5 of the band's songs. I studied those songs like crazy, playing them over and over again.

Chuck introduced me to Mike, the bass player, and Scotty, the drummer. All of these guys were older than me by about ten years. So, I was a little intimidated. I had never been in a "real" band before. I had played in some goofy jam bands with my high school buddies, but we never played any shows in front of actual people.

We started off by playing one of the slower songs from the demo CD as a kind of warm-up for the whole band. The song had a very intricate and pretty clean guitar intro. The band originally only had three members meaning Chuck had to fill the sonic space on his own with just the one guitar. So, his guitar riffs were often written to be big and sprawling. Which meant I had to find some way to fit in with those parts.

The band started the song, and I watched what Chuck was playing on his guitar. It was far more complicated than I had originally thought. So I played my version of what I had learned by ear. It was basically a stripped-down and simplified version of what Chuck was playing. But it worked. My simplistic style complemented and rounded out Chuck's intricate guitar melody.

The verse of the song was much the same. However, Chuck sang and played a more complex riff while I played a simplified version of that.

Then, the chorus came in. We stomped on our distortion pedals, and I knew it was my time to shine. Chuck didn't know that I had a few tricks up my sleeve. When he went to a more simplified chord progression for the catchy chorus, I played a part that I had written while listening to the song on my own.

Scotty and Mike were impressed. I instinctively knew when to step back and let Chuck's playing and singing take center stage, and I knew that when he throttled back, I was able to add in my own flair.

I added in the vocal harmony parts over Chuck's vocal melody during that chorus. Chuck looked over at me with surprise in his eyes. He certainly wasn't expecting me to have come up with vocal harmonies. Luckily, they sounded pretty good, too. Chuck's voice is a fair bit deeper in pitch than mine, so my vocal harmonies sat naturally in a higher range. It was a perfect balance.

It all came together beautifully. The rest of the songs went much the same way as the first. I did my best to find a spot in each song to fit in, step back, or step up.

After we finished running through all the songs, I started plucking around on my guitar with a quiet, clean sound. I didn't think much of it, just something to keep my hands occupied while the guys talked about when we would be ready for our first gig. Then, Mike stopped the conversation and asked me to play it again. I obliged, and Chuck asked me to just keep playing it over and over.

Again, I'm not the fanciest or most technical player, so the riff I was playing was simple and catchy. But Chuck felt like it was building up to something. So, he played some atmospheric notes. Scotty and Mike followed suit, coming up with rhythm parts that felt like going up and up and up on a roller coaster.

I stomped on my distortion pedal and started playing the first four power chords that came to mind. They were big, powerful, and sprawling, the perfect explosion to follow that epic build-up. Chuck loved it. I showed Mike the progression, and he locked his bass in with my progression. Scotty didn't miss a beat and slammed on his drums. Our first song written together, as a band, transported us to another place entirely.

Everything I had learned on my own about music and playing guitar all clicked into place simultaneously in that little rehearsal room with Chuck, Scotty, and Mike. One foot in front of the other that eventually led me to exactly where I needed to be.

I've been playing guitar for over 16 years, and I often joke that I should be better at it than I actually am. But I love what I play, and I wouldn't change a thing. At this point in my life, to not play guitar would be comparable to losing a limb. It's become such an important part of who I am that I couldn't imagine it going any other way.

About the Expert

Norm Fernandez is a freelance writer specializing in blog content, marketing, copywriting, and video scripts. He founded Fernandez Freelance Writing, LLC.to help as many people and businesses as he can with his writing. Norm also part-time coaches CrossFit and Olympic Weightlifting. He has played guitar for over 15 years in several local bands all across southwest Florida, and he continues to rock out crowds to this day.

HowExpert publishes quick 'how to' guides by everyday experts. Visit HowExpert.com to learn more.

Recommended Resources

- HowExpert.com – Quick 'How To' Guides on All Topics from A to Z by Everyday Experts.
- HowExpert.com/free – Free HowExpert Email Newsletter.
- HowExpert.com/books – HowExpert Books
- HowExpert.com/courses – HowExpert Courses
- HowExpert.com/clothing – HowExpert Clothing
- HowExpert.com/membership – HowExpert Membership Site
- HowExpert.com/affiliates – HowExpert Affiliate Program
- HowExpert.com/jobs – HowExpert Jobs
- HowExpert.com/writers – Write About Your #1 Passion/Knowledge/Expertise & Become a HowExpert Author.
- HowExpert.com/resources – Additional HowExpert Recommended Resources
- YouTube.com/HowExpert – Subscribe to HowExpert YouTube.
- Instagram.com/HowExpert – Follow HowExpert on Instagram.
- Facebook.com/HowExpert – Follow HowExpert on Facebook.
- TikTok.com/@HowExpert – Follow HowExpert on TikTok.

www.ingramcontent.com/pod-product-compliance
Lightning Source LLC
LaVergne TN
LVHW091552060526
838200LV00036B/798